THE NETWORK OF THOUGHT

*Authentic Report of Talks in 1981 in
Saanen, Switzerland, and Amsterdam, Holland*

J. Krishnamurti

THE NETWORK
OF THOUGHT

second edition

mirananda

For more information
please write to:

Krishnamurti Foundation Trust
Brockwood Park, Bramdean
Hampshire SO24 0LQ, U.K.

CIP-GEGEVENS KONINKLIJKE BIBLIOTHEEK, DEN HAAG

Krishnamurti, J.

The network of thought / J. Krishnamurti. – [Wassenaar] :
Mirananda
Lezingen gehouden in Saanen (Zwitserland) en Amsterdam in
1981.
ISBN 90-6271-675-X
SISO 281 UDC 141 UGI 556
Trefw.: oosterse filosofie.

ISBN 90 6271 675 X

CONTENTS

1

I see some of my old friends are here — and I am glad to see you. As we are going to have seven talks we should go into what I am going to say very carefully, covering the whole field of life, so please be patient those of you who have heard the speaker before, please be tolerant if the speaker repeats himself, for repetition has a certain value.

Prejudice has something in common with ideals, beliefs and faiths. We must be able to think together; but our prejudices, our ideals and so on, limit the capacity and the energy required to think, to observe and examine together so as to discover for ourselves what lies behind all the confusion, misery, terror, destruction and tremendous violence in the world. To understand, not only the mere outward facts that are taking place, but also the depth and the significance of all this, we must be able to observe together — not you observing one way and the speaker another, but together observe the same thing. That observation, that examination, is prevented if we cling to our prejudices, to our particular experiences and our particular comprehension. Thinking together is tremendously important because we have to face a world that is rapidly disintegrating, degenerating, a world in which there is no sense of morality, where nothing is sacred, where no one respects another. To understand all this, not only superficially, casually, we have to enter into the depths of it, into what lies behind it. We have to enquire why it is that after all these millions of years of evolution, man, you and the whole world, have become so violent, callous, destructive, enduring wars and the atomic bomb. The technological world is evolving more and more; perhaps that may be one of the factors causing man to become like this. So, please let us think together, not according to my way or your way, but simply using the capacity to think.

Thought is the common factor of all mankind. There is no Eastern thought, or Western thought; there is only the common capacity to think, whether one is utterly poor or most sophisticated, living in an affluent society. Whether a surgeon, a carpenter, a labourer in the field, or a great poet, thought is the common factor of all of us. We do not seem to realise that thought is the common factor that binds us all. You think according to your capacity, to your energy, your experience and knowledge; another thinks differently according to his experience and conditioning. We are all caught in this network of thought. This is a fact, indisputable and actual.

We have been 'programmed' biologically, physically and also 'programmed' mentally, intellectually. We must be aware of having been programmed, like a computer. Computers are programmed by experts to produce the results that they want. And these computers will outstrip man in thought. These computers can gather experience, and from that experience learn, accumulate knowledge, according to their programme. Gradually they are going to outstrip all our thinking in accuracy and with greater speed. Of course they cannot compose as Beethoven, or as Keats, but they will outstrip our thinking.

So, then, what is man? He has been programmed to be Catholic, Protestant, to be Italian or British and so on. For centuries he has been programmed — to believe, to have faith, to follow certain rituals, certain dogmas; programmed to be nationalistic and to go to war. So his brain has become as a computer but not so capable because his thought is limited, whereas the computer, although being also limited, is able to think much more rapidly than the human being and can outstrip him.

These are facts, this is what actually is going on. Then what becomes of man? Then what is man? If the robots and the computer can do almost all that the human being can do, then what is the future society of man? When cars can be built by the robot and the computer — probably much better — then what is going to become of man as a social entity? These and many other problems are facing us. You cannot any more think as Christians, Buddhists, Hindus and Muslims. We are facing a tremendous crisis; a crisis which the politicians can never solve because they are programmed to think in a particular way — nor can the scientists understand or solve the crisis; nor yet the business world, the world of money. The turning point, the perceptive decision, the challenge, is not in politics, in religion, in the scientific world, it is in our consciousness. One has to understand the consciousness of mankind, which has brought us to this point. One has to be very serious about this matter because we are really facing something very dangerous in the world — where there is the proliferation of the atomic bomb which some lunatic will turn on. We all must be aware of all this.

One has to be very very serious, not flippant, not casual but concerned, to understand this behaviour and how human thought has brought us all to this point. We must be able to penetrate very carefully, hesitantly, with deep observation, to understand together what is happening both out there and inwardly. The inward psychological activity always overcomes the outer, however many regulations, sanctions, decisions you may have outwardly, all these are shattered by our psychological desires, fears and anxieties, by the longing for security. Unless we understand that, whatever outward semblance of order we may have, inward disorder always overcomes that which is outwardly conforming, disciplined, regularised. There may be carefully constructed institutions — political, religious, economic —but whatever the construction of these may be, unless our inward consciousness is in total order, inward disorder will always overcome the outer. We have seen this historically, it is happening now in front of our eyes. This is a fact.

The turning point is in our consciousness. Our consciousness is a very complicated affair. Volumes have been written about it, both in the East and in the West. We are not aware of our own consciousness; to examine that consciousness in all its complexity one has to be free to look, to be choicelessly aware of its movement. It is not that the speaker is directing you to look or to listen to all the inward movement of consciousness in a particular way. Consciousness is common to all mankind.Throughout the world man suffers inwardly as well as outwardly there is anxiety, uncertainty, utter despair of loneliness; there is insecurity, jealousy, greed, envy and suffering. Human consciousness is one whole; it is not your consciousness or mine. This is logical, sane, rational: wherever you go, in whatever climate you live, whether you are affluent or degradingly poor, whether you believe in god, or in some other entity, belief and faith are common to all mankind — the images and symbols may be totally different in various localities but they stem from something common to all mankind. This is not a mere verbal statement. If you take it as a verbal statement, as an idea, as a concept, then you will not see the deep significance involved in it. The significance is that your consciousness is the consciousness of all humanity because you suffer, you are anxious, you are lonely, insecure, confused, exactly like others, though they live ten thousand miles away. The realisation of it, the feeling of it — the feeling in your guts — is totally different from the mere verbal acceptance. When you realise that you are the rest of mankind, it brings a tremendous energy, you have broken through the narrow groove of individuality, the narrow circle of me and you, we and they. We are examining together this very complex consciousness of man, not the European man, not the Asiatic man or the Middle East man, but this extraordinary movement in time that has been going on in consciousness for millions of years.

Please do not accept what the speaker is saying; if you do it will have no meaning. If you do not begin to doubt, begin to question, be sceptical to enquire, if you hold on to your own particular belief, faith, experience or the accumulated knowledge, then you will reduce it all to some kind of pettiness with very little meaning. If you do that you will not be facing the tremendous issue that is facing man.

We have to see what our actual consciousness is. Thought and all the things that thought has put together, is part of our consciousness — the culture in which we live, the aesthetic values, the economic pressures, the national inheritance. If you are a surgeon or a carpenter, if you specialize in a particular profession, that group consciousness is part of your consciousness. If you live in a particular country with its particular tradition and religious culture, that particular group-consciousness has become part of your consciousness. These are facts. If you are a carpenter you have to have certain skills, understand the nature of wood and the tools of the trade, so you gradually belong to a group that has cultivated these special skills and that has its own consciousness —

similarly the scientist, the archeologist, just as the animals have their own particular consciousness as a group. If you are a housewife you have your own particular group-consciousness, like all the other housewives. Permissiveness has spread throughout the world; it began in the far West and has spread right through the world. That is a group-conscious movement. See the significance of it; go into it for yourself, see what is involved in it.

Our consciousness includes, in the much deeper consciousness, our fears. Man has lived with fear for generation after generation. He has lived with pleasure, with envy, with all the travail of loneliness, depression and confusion; and with great sorrow, with what he calls love and the everlasting fear of death. All this is his consciousness which is common to all mankind. Realise what it means: it means that you are no longer an individual. This is very hard to accept because we have been programmed, as is the computer, to think we are individuals. We have been programmed religiously to think that we have souls separate from all the others. Being programmed our brain works in the same pattern century after century.

If one understands the nature of our consciousness, then the particular endeavour of the 'me' that suffers has become something global, then a totally different activity will take place. That is the crisis we are in. We have been programmed; being programmed we can learn — occasionally have an insight — and our brain repeats itself over and over again. Just see the actual fact of that: one is a Christian, or a Buddhist or a Hindu; one is against Communism, one is a Communist or a Democrat, repeat, repeat, repeat. And in this state of repetition there is an occasional break-through.

So, how shall a human being — who is actually the rest of mankind — how shall he face this crisis, this turning point? How will you as a human being, who has evolved through millenia upon millenia, thinking as an individual — which is actually an illusion — face a turning point, see what actually is and in that very perception move totally in another direction?

Let us understand together what it means to look — to look at the actuality of thought. You all think, that is why you are here. You all think and thought expresses itself in words, or through a gesture, through a look, through some bodily movement. Words being common to each one of us, we understand through those words the significance of what is being said. Yet thought is common to all mankind — it is a most extraordinary thing if you have discovered that, for then you see that thought is not your thought, it is thought. We have to learn how to see things as they actually are — not as you are programmed to look. See the difference. Can we be free of being programmed and look? If you look as a Christian, a Democrat, a Communist, a Socialist or a Catholic or a Protestant — which are all so many prejudices — then you will not be able to understand the enormity of the danger, the crisis, that we are facing. If you belong to a certain group, or follow a certain guru, or are committed to a certain form of action, then, because you have been programmed, you will be incapable of looking at things as they actually are. It is only if you do not belong to any organization, to any group, to any particular religion or nationality, that you can really observe. If you have accumulated a great deal of knowledge from books and from experience, your mind has already been filled, your brain is crowded with experience, with your particular tendencies and so on — all that is going to prevent you from looking. Can we be free of all that to look at what is actually happening in the world? — at the terror and the terrible religious sectarian divisions, one guru opposed to another idiotic guru, the vanity behind all that, the power, the position, the wealth of these gurus, it is appalling. Can you look at yourself — not as a separate human being but as a human being who is actually the rest of mankind? To have such a feeling means that you have tremendous love for human beings.

When you are able to see clearly, without any distortion, then you begin to enquire into the nature of consciousness, including the much deeper layers of consciousness. You have to enquire into the whole movement of thought, because it is thought that is responsible for all the content of consciousness, whether it is the deep or the superficial layers. If you had no thought there would be no fear, no sense of pleasure, no time; thought is responsible. Thought is responsible for the beauty of a great cathedral, but thought is also responsible for all the nonsense that takes place inside the cathedral. All the achievements of the great painters, poets, composers, are the activity of thought: the composer; inwardly hearing the marvellous sound, commits it onto paper. That is the movement of thought. Thought is responsible for all the gods in the world, all the saviours, all the gurus; for all the obedience and devotion; the whole is the result of thought which seeks gratification and escape from loneliness. Thought is the common factor of all mankind. The poorest villager in India thinks as the chief executive thinks, as the religious leader thinks. That is a common everyday fact. That is the ground on which all human beings stand. You cannot escape from that.

Thought has done marvellous things to help man but it has also brought about great destruction and terror in the world. We have to understand the nature and the

14

movement of thought; why you think in a certain way; why you cling to certain forms of thought; why you hold on to certain experiences; why thought has never understood the nature of death. We have to examine the very structure of thought — not your thought because it is fairly obvious what your thought is, for you have been programmed. But if you enquire seriously into what thinking is, then you enter into quite a different dimension — not the dimension of your own particular little problem. You must understand the tremendous movement of thought, the nature of thinking — not as a philosopher, not as a religious man, not as a member of a particular profession, or a housewife — the enormous vitality of thinking.

Thought is responsible for all the cruelty, the wars, the war machines and the brutality of war, the killing, the terror, the throwing of bombs, the taking of hostages in the name of a cause, or without a cause. Thought is also responsible for the cathedrals, the beauty of their structure, the lovely poems; it is also responsible for all the technological development, the computer with its extraordinary capacity to learn and go beyond man's thought. What is thinking? It is a response, a reaction, of memory. If you had no memory you would not be able to think. Memory is stored in the brain as knowledge, the result of experience. This is how our brain operates. First, experience; that experience may have been from the beginning of man, which we have inherited, that experience gives knowledge which is stored up in the brain; from knowledge there is memory and from that memory thought. From thought you act. From that action you learn more. So you repeat the cycle. Experience, knowledge, memory, thought, action; from that action learn more and repeat. This is how we are programmed. We are always doing this: having remembered pain, in the future avoid pain by not doing the thing that will cause pain, which becomes knowledge, and repeat that. Sexual pleasure, repeat that. This is the movement of thought. See the beauty of it, how mechanically thought operates. Thought says to itself: 'I am free to operate.' Yet thought is never free because it is based on knowledge and knowledge is obviously always limited. Knowledge must also be always limited because it is part of time. I will learn more and to learn more I must have time. I do not know Russian but I will learn it. It may take me six months or a year or a lifetime. Knowledge is the movement of time. Time, knowledge, thought and action; in this cycle we live. Thought is limited, so whatever action thought generates must be limited and such limitation must create conflict, must be divisive.

If I say that I am a Hindu, that I am Indian, I am limited and that limitation brings about not only corruption but conflict because another says, 'I am a Christian' or 'I am a Buddhist', so there is conflict between us. Our life from birth to death is a series of struggles and conflicts from which we are always trying to escape, which again causes more conflict. We live and die in this perpetual and endless conflict. We never seek out the root of that conflict, which is thought, because thought is limited. Please do not ask, 'How am I to stop thought?' — that is not the point. The point is to understand the nature of thought, to look at it.

12th July, 1981

16

2

We were saying that human consciousness is similar in all human beings. Our consciousness, whether we live in the East or West, is made up of many layers of fears, anxieties, pleasures, sorrows and every form of faith. Occasionally, perhaps, in that consciousness there is also love, compassion, and from that compassion a totally different kind of intelligence. And always there is the fear of ending, death. Human beings throughout the world from time immemorial have tried to find out if there is something sacred, beyond all thought, something incorruptible and timeless.

There are the various group consciousnesses; the businessmen with their consciousness, the scientists with theirs and the carpenter with his, these are of the content of consciousness and are the product of thought. Thought has created wonderful things; from the extraordinary technology of computers, to telecommunication, to robots, surgery and medicine. Thought has invented religions; all the religious organizations throughout the world are put together by thought.

Thought has invented the computer. You must understand the complexity and the future of the computer; it is going to outstrip man in his thought; it is going to change the structure of society and the structure of government. This is not some fantastic conclusion of the speaker, or some fantasy, it is something that is actually going on now, of which you may not be aware. The computer has a mechanical intelligence; it can learn and invent. The computer is going to make human labour practically unnecessary — perhaps two hours work a day. These are all changes that are coming. You may not like it, you may revolt against it, but it is coming.

Thought has invented the computer, but human thought is limited and the mechanical intelligence of the computer is going beyond that of man. It is going to totally revolutionize our lives. So what will a human being be then? These are facts, not some specialized conclusions of the speaker.

When we consider what the capacity of the computer is, then we have to ask ourselves: what is a human being to do? The computer is going to take over most of the activities of the brain. And what happens to the brain then? When a human being's occupation is taken over by the computer, by the robot, what becomes of the human? We human beings have been 'programmed' biologically, intellectually, emotionally, psychologically, through millions of years, and we repeat the pattern of the programme over and over again. We have stopped learning: and we must enquire if the human brain, which has been programmed for so many centuries, is capable of learning and immediately transforming itself into a totally different dimension. If we are not capable of that, the computer, which is much more capable, rapid and accurate, is going to take over the activities of the brain. This is not something casual, this is a very very serious, desperately serious matter. The computer can invent a new religion. It could be programmed by an expert Hindu scholar, by a Catholic, by a Protestant or a Muslim, and it would turn out a marvellous structure for a new religion! And we, if we are not aware of what is happening, we will follow that new structure which has been turned out by the computer. See the seriousness of all this, please.

Our consciousness has been programmed for thousands and thousands of years to think of ourselves as individuals, as separate entities struggling, in conflict from the moment we are born until we die. We are programmed to that. We have accepted that. We have never challenged it; we have never asked if it is possible to live a life absolutely without conflict. Never having asked it we will never learn about it. We repeat. It is an innate part of our existence to be in conflict — nature is in conflict: that is our argument — and we consider that progress is only through conflict. Religious organizations throughout history have maintained the idea of individual salvation. We are questioning very seriously whether there is an individual consciousness; whether you, as a human being, have a separate consciousness from the rest of mankind. You have to answer this, not just play with it.

Having been brought up, programmed, conditioned, to be individuals, then our consciousness is all this activity of thought. Fear and the pursuit of pleasure are the movement of thought. The suffering, anxiety, uncertainty and the deep regrets, wounds, the burden of centuries of sorrow, are all part of thought. Thought is responsible for what we call love, which has become sensual pleasure, something to be desired.

As we said, and we will repeat it over and over again until we are quite sure of it, we are thinking together, the speaker is not telling you what to think. He is not making propaganda — it is a horrible thing, propaganda. He is not telling you how to act, what to believe, but together, we are investigating the catastrophe that is taking place in the world outside of us, the utter ruthlessness and violence, and also inwardly in each human being the extraordinary conflict that is going on. Together we are

19

examining. It is not — if one may point out — that you are merely listening to some ideas or conclusions; we are not talking about ideas, conclusions or beliefs. We are looking at this world that human beings have produced, for which all of us are responsible. We must be clear in our understanding — at whatever level that understanding be, whether it is intellectual understanding, which is merely verbal, or the understanding of deep significance so that that understanding acts — that we have come to a point where we have to make a decision, not by the exercise of will, but the decision that will naturally come when we begin to understand the whole nature and structure of the world, both externally and internally. That perception will bring about a decision, an action.

Thought has created the problems which surround us and our brains are trained, educated, conditioned, to the solving of problems. Thought has created the problems, like the division between nationalities. Thought has created the division and the conflict between various economic structures; thought has created the various religions and the divisions between them and therefore there is conflict. The brain is trained to attempt to solve these conflicts which thought has created. It is essential that we understand deeply the nature of our thinking and the nature of our reactions which arise from our thinking. Thought dominates our lives, whatever we do; whatever action takes place, thought is behind that action. In every activity, whether it is sensual or intellectual, or biological, thought is operating all the time. Biologically, through centuries, the brain has been programmed, conditioned — the body acts in its own way, the action of breathing, the beat of the heart and so on — so, if you are a Catholic, a Hindu, or a Buddhist, you repeat that conditioning over and over again.

Thought is a movement in time and space. Thought is memory, the remembrance of past things. Thought is the activity of knowledge, knowledge which has been gathered together through millions of years and stored as memory in the brain. If you observe the activity of your thinking you will see that experience and knowledge are the basis of your life. Knowledge is never complete, it must always go together with ignorance. We think knowledge is going to solve all our problems, whether the knowledge of the priest, the guru, the scientist, the philosopher, or the latest psychiatrist. But we have never questioned whether knowledge in itself can solve any of our problems — exept perhaps technological problems.

Knowledge comes through time. To learn a language you need time. To learn a skill or to drive a car efficiently takes time. The same movement of time is brought over to the psychological field; there too we say, 'I must have time to learn about myself.' 'I must have time in order to change myself from 'what I am' to 'what I should be.' Bringing over the activity of the external world into the psychological world means that time is a great factor in our life — tomorrow, the past and the present. Time is thought. Time is required in the acquisition of knowledge through experience, both externally in the world and inwardly. That is the way we have been programmed.

Being so programmed we consider time is necessary to bring about a deep, fundamental change in the human structure. We employ time as thought — 'I am this, I shall be that.' You would also say in the technical world: 'I do not know how to construct a computer but I will learn.' Time, knowledge, memory, thought, they are a single unit; they are not separate activities but a single movement. Thought, the outcome of knowledge, must everlastingly be incomplete and therefore limited, because knowledge is incomplete. Whatever is limited must bring about conflict. Nationality is limited. Religious belief is limited. An experience which you have had, or which you are longing for, is limited. Every experience must be limited.

Questioner: Why?

KRISHNAMURTI: Because there are more experiences. I may have an experience sexually, or the experience of the possession of wealth, the experience of giving everything up and going into a monastery — those experiences are all limited.

Thought, being limited, creates problems — national, economic and religious divisions; then thought says, 'I must solve them.' So thought is always functioning in the resolution of problems. And the computer, a mechanism which has been programmed, can outstrip all of us because it has no problems; it evolves, learns, moves.

Our consciousness has been programmed as an individual consciousness. We are questioning whether that consciousness, which we have accepted as individual, is actually individual at all. Do not say: 'What will happen if I am not an individual?' Something totally different may happen. You may have an individual training in a particular trade, in a particular profession, you may be a surgeon, a doctor, an engineer, but that does not make you an individual. You may have a different name, a different form — that does not make individuality; nor the acceptance that the brain through time has affirmed: 'I am an individual, it is my desire to fulfil, to become through struggle.' That so-called individual consciousness, which is yours, is the consciousness of all humanity.

If your consciousness, which you have accepted as

22

separate, is not separate, then what is the nature of your consciousness? Part of it is the sensory responses. Those sensory responses are naturally, necessarily, programmed to defend yourself, through hunger to seek food, to breathe, unconsciously. Biologically you are programmed. Then the content of your consciousness includes the many hurts and wounds that you have received from childhood, the many forms of guilt; it includes the various ideas, imaginary certainties; the many experiences, both sensory and psychological; there is always the basis, the root, of fear in its many forms. With fear naturally goes hatred. Where there is fear there must be violence, aggression, the tremendous urge to succeed, both in the physical and the psychological world. In the content of consciousness there is the constant pursuit of pleasure; the pleasure of possession, of domination, the pleasure of money which gives power, the pleasure of a philosopher with his immense knowledge, the guru with his circus. Pleasure again has innumerable forms. There is also pain, anxiety, the deep sense of abiding loneliness and sorrow, not only the so-called personal sorrow but also the enormous sorrow brought about through wars, through neglect, through this endless conquering of one group of people by another. In that consciousness there is the racial and group content; ultimately there is death.

This is our consciousness — beliefs, certainties and uncertainties, anxiety, loneliness and endless misery. These are the facts. And we say this consciousness is mine! Is that so? Go to the Far East, or the Near East, America, Europe, anywhere where human beings are; they suffer, they are anxious, lonely, depressed, melancholic, struggling and in conflict — they are just the same as you. So, is your consciousness different from that of another? I know it is very difficult for people to accept —

23

you may logically accept it, intellectually you may say, 'Yes, that is so, maybe.' But to feel this total human sense that you are the rest of mankind requires a great deal of sensitivity. It is not a problem to be solved. It is not that you must accept that you are not an individual, that you must endeavour to feel this global human entity. If you do, you have made it into a problem which the brain is only too ready to try to solve! But if you really look at it with your mind, your heart, your whole being totally aware of this fact, then you have broken the programme. It is naturally broken. But if you say, 'I will break it,' then you are again back into the same pattern. To the speaker this is utter reality, not something verbally accepted because it is pleasant; it is something that is actual. You may have logically, reasonably and sanely examined and found that it is so; but the brain which has been programmed to the sense of individuality is going to revolt against it (which you are doing now). The brain is unwilling to learn. Whereas the computer will learn because it has nothing to lose. But here you are frightened of losing something.

Can the brain learn? That is the whole point; so now we have to go into this question of what learning is. Learning Learning for most of us is a process of acquiring knowledge. I do not know the Russian language but I will learn it. I will learn day after day, memorizing, holding on to certain words, phrases and the meanings, syntax and grammar. If I apply myself I can learn almost any language within a certain time. To us, learning is essentially the accumulation of knowledge or skill. Our brains are conditioned to this pattern. Accumulate knowledge and from that act. When I learn a language, there knowledge is necessary. But if I am learning psychologically about the content of my mind, of my consciousness, does learning there imply examining each layer of it and accumulating knowledge about it and from that knowledge acting — following the same pattern as learning a language? If the brain repeats that pattern when I am learning about the content of my consciousness, it means that I need time to accumulate knowledge about myself, my consciousness. Then I determine what the problems are and the brain is ready to solve them — it has been trained to solve problems. It is repeating this endless pattern and that is what I call learning. Is there a learning which is not this? Is there a different action of learning, which is not the accumulation of knowledge? You understand the difference?

Let me put it differently: from experience we acquire knowledge, from knowledge memory; the response of memory is thought, then from thought action, from that action you learn more, so the cycle is repeated. That is the pattern of our life. That form of learning will never solve our problems because it is repetition. We acquire more knowledge which may lead to better action; but that action is limited and this we keep repeating. The activity from that knowledge will not solve our human problems at all. We have not solved them, it is so obvious. After millions of years we have not solved our problems: we are cutting each other's throats, we are competing with each other, we hate each other, we want to be successful, the whole pattern is repeated from the time man began and we are still at it. Do what you will along this pattern and no human problem will be solved, whether it be political, religious or economic, because it is thought that is operating.

Now, is there another form of learning; learning, not in the context of knowledge, but a different form, a non-accumulative perception-action? To find out we have to enquire whether it is possible to observe the content of our consciousness and to observe the world without a single prejudice. Is that possible? Do not say it is not possible, just ask the question. See whether, when you have a prejudice, you can observe clearly. You cannot, obviously. If you have a certain conclusion, a certain set of beliefs, concepts, ideals, and you want to see clearly what the world is, all those conclusions, ideals, prejudices and so on will actually prevent it. It is not a question of how to get rid of your prejudices but of seeing clearly, intelligently, that any form of prejudice, however noble or ignoble will actually prevent perception. When you see that, prejudices go. What is important is not the prejudice but the demand to see clearly.

If I want to be a good surgeon I cannot do so with ideals or prejudices about surgeons; I must actually perform surgery. Can you see that a new form of action, a new form of non-accumulative knowledge, is possible which will break the pattern, break the programme, so that you are acting totally differently?

The way we have lived, over millions of years, has been the repetition of the same process of acquiring knowledge and acting from that knowledge. That knowledge and action is limited. That limitation creates problems and the brain has become accustomed to solving the problems which knowledge has repeatedly created. The brain is caught in that pattern and we are saying that that pattern will never, in any circumstance, solve our human problems. Obviously we have not solved them up till now. There must be a different, a totally different, movement, which is a non-accumulative perception-action. To have non-accumulative perception is to have no prejudice. It is to have absolutely no ideals, no concepts, no faith — because all those have destroyed man, they have not solved his problems.

26

So: have you a prejudice? Have you a prejudice which has something in common with an ideal? Of course. Ideals are to be accomplished in the future, and knowledge becomes tremendously important in the realising of ideals. So, can you observe without accumulation, without the destructive nature of prejudice, ideals, faith, belief and your own conclusions and experiences? There is group consciousness, national consciousness, linguistic consciousness, professional consciousness, racial consciousness, and there is fear, anxiety, sorrow, loneliness, the pursuit of pleasure, love and finally death. If you keep acting in that circle, you maintain the human consciousness of the world. Just see the truth of this. You are part of that consciousness and you sustain it by saying, 'I am an individual. My prejudices are important. My ideals are essential' — repeating the same thing over and over again. Now the maintenance, the sustenance and the nourishment, of that consciousness takes place when you are repeating that pattern. But when you break away from that consciousness, you are introducing a totally new factor in the whole of that consciousness.

Now, if we understand the nature of our own consciousness, if we see how it is operating in this endless cycle of knowledge, action and division — a consciousness which has been sustained for millenia — if we see the truth that all this is a form of prejudice and break away from it, we introduce a new factor into the old. It means that you, as a human being who is of the consciousness of the rest of mankind, can move away from the old pattern of obedience and acceptance. That is the real turning point in your life. Man cannot go on repeating the old pattern, it has lost its meaning — in the psychological world it has totally lost its meaning. If you fulfil yourself, who cares? If you become a saint, what does it matter?

Whereas, if you totally move away from that you affect the whole consciousness of mankind.

14th July, 1981

3

I would like to repeat that we are not trying to convince you of anything — that must be clearly understood. We are not trying to persuade you to accept a particular point of view. We are not trying to impress you about anything; nor are we doing any propaganda. We are not talking about personalities, or who is right and who is wrong, but rather trying to think out, to observe, together, what the world is and what we are, what we have made of the world and what we have made of ourselves. We are trying together to examine both the inward and the outward man.

To observe clearly one must be free to look — obviously. If one clings to one's particular experiences, judgements and prejudices, then it is not possible to think clearly. The world crisis which is right in front of us demands, urges, that we think together so that we can solve the human problem together, not according to any particular person, philosopher, or particular guru. We are trying to observe together. It is important to bear in mind all the time that the speaker is merely pointing out something which we are examining together. It is not something one-sided but rather that we are co-operating in examining, in taking a journey together and so acting together.

It is very important to understand that our consciousness is not our individual consciousness. Our consciousness is not only that of the specialized group, nationality and so on, but it is also all the human travail, conflict, misery, confusion and sorrow. We are examining together that human consciousness, which is our consciousness, not yours or mine, but ours.

One of the factors that is demanded in this examination is the capacity of intelligence. Intelligence is the capacity to discern, to understand, to distinguish; it is also the capacity to observe, to put together all that we have gathered and to act from that. That gathering, that discernment, that observation, can be prejudiced; and intelligence is denied when there is prejudice. If you follow another, intelligence is denied; the following of another, however noble, denies your own perception, denies your own observation — you are merely following somebody who will tell you what to do, what to think. If you do that, then intelligence does not exist; because in that there is no observation and therefore no intelligence. Intelligence demands doubting, questioning, not being impressed by others, by their enthusiasm, by their energy. Intelligence demands that there be impersonal observation. Intelligence is not only the capacity to understand that which is rationally, verbally explained but also implies that we gather as much information as possible, yet knowing that that information can never be complete, about anybody or anything. Where there is intelligence there is hesitation, observation and the clarity of rational impersonal thinking. The comprehension of the whole of man, of all his complexities, all his physical responses, his emotional reactions, his intellectual capacities, his affection and his travail, the perceiving of all that at one glance, in one act, is supreme intelligence. Intelligence has not, so far, been able to transcend conflict. We are going together to see if it is possible for the brain to be free from conflict. We live with conflict from the time

30

we are born and will continue to do so until we die. There is the constant struggle to be, to become something spiritually, so-called, or psychologically; to become successful in the world; to fulfil — all that is the movement of becoming: I am this now but I will reach the ultimate destination, the highest principle, whether that principle be called god, Brahman, or any other name. The constant struggle whether to become, or to be, is the same. But when one is trying to become, in various directions, then you are denying being. When you try to be you are becoming also. See this movement of the mind, of thought: I think I am, and being dissatisfied, discontented, with what I am, I try to fulfil myself in something; I drive towards a particular goal; it may be painful, but the end is thought to be pleasurable. There is this constant struggle to be and to become.

We are all trying to become; physically, we want a better house, a better position with more power, higher status. Biologically, if we are not well we seek to become well. Psychologically, the whole inward process of thought, of consciousness, the whole drive, inwardly, is from the recognition that one is actually nothing, and by becoming, to move away from that. Psychologically, inwardly, there is always the escape from 'what is', always the running away from that which I am, from that with which I am dissatisfied to something which will satisfy me. Whether that satisfaction is conceived as deep contentment, happiness, or enlightenment, which is a projection of thought, or as acquiring greater knowledge, it is still the process of becoming — I am, I shall be. That process involves time. The brain is 'programmed' to this. All our culture, all our religious sanctions, everything says: 'become'. It is a phenomenon to be seen all over the world. Not only in this Western world but in the East, everyone is trying to become, or to be, or to avoid. Now: is this the cause of conflict, inwardly and outwardly? Inwardly there is this imitation, competition, conformity with the ideal; outwardly there is this competition between so-called individuals of one group against another group, nation against nation. Inwardly and outwardly there is always this drive to become and to be something.

We are asking: is this the basic cause of our conflict? Is man doomed — as long as he lives on this marvellous earth — to perpetual conflict? One can rationalize this conflict, say nature is in conflict, the tree struggling to reach the sun is in conflict, and that that is part of our nature, because, through conflict, through competition, we have evolved, we have grown into this marvellous human being that we are — this is not being said sarcastically. Our brain is programmed to conflict. We have a problem which we have never been able to resolve. You may neurotically escape into some phantasy and in that phantasy be totally content, or you may imagine that you have inwardly achieved something and be totally content with that: an intelligent mind must question all this, it must exercise doubt, scepticism. Why have human beings, for millions of years, from the beginning of man up to the present time, lived in conflict? We have accepted it, we have tolerated it, we have said it is part of our nature to compete, to be aggressive, to imitate, to conform; we have said that it is part of the everlasting pattern of life.

Why is man, who is so highly sophisticated in one direction, so utterly unintelligent in other directions? Does conflict end through knowledge — knowledge about oneself, or about the world, knowledge about matter, learning more about society so as to have better organizations and better institutions, acquiring more and more knowledge? Will that solve our human conflict? Or

32

is it that freedom from conflict has nothing whatsoever to do with knowledge?

We have a great deal of knowledge about the world, about matter and the universe; we have also a great deal of historical knowledge about ourselves: will that knowledge free the human being from conflict? Or has freedom from conflict nothing to do with analysis, with discovering the various causes and factors of conflict? Will analytical discovery of the cause, or many causes, free the brain from conflict — the conflict which we have while we are awake during the daytime and the conflict carried on while we are asleep? We can examine and interpret dreams, we can go into the whole question of why human beings dream at all; will that solve conflict? Will the analytical mind analysing very clearly, rationally, sanely into the cause of conflict, end conflict? In analysis the analyser tries to analyse conflict, and in doing so separates himself from conflict — will that solve it? Or is it that freedom has nothing whatsoever to do with any of these processes? If you follow somebody who says: 'I will show you the way; I am free from conflict and I will show you the way' — will that help you? This has been the part of the priest, the part of the guru, the part of the so-called enlightened man — 'Follow me, I will show you;' or, 'I will point out the goal to you.' History shows this through millenia upon millenia, and yet man has not been able to solve his deep-rooted conflict.

Let us find out together — not agree, not as an intellectual verbal concept — if there is a perception, an action, that will end conflict, not gradually, but immediately. What are the implications of that? The brain being programmed to conflict is caught in that pattern. We are asking if that pattern can be broken immediately, not gradually. You may think you can break it through drugs, through alcohol, through sex, through different forms of discipline, through handing oneself over to something — man has tried a thousand different ways to escape from this terror of conflict. Now, we are asking: is it possible for a conditioned brain to break that conditioning immediately? This may be a theoretical, non-actual, question. You may say it is impossible, it is just a theory, it is just a wish, a desire, to be free of this conflict. But if you examine the matter rationally, logically, with intelligence, you see that time will not solve this conditioning. The first thing to realise is that there is no psychological tomorrow. If you see actually, not verbally, but deeply in your heart, in your mind, in the very very depths of your being, you will realise that time will not solve this problem. And that means that you have already broken the pattern, you have begun to see cracks in the pattern we have accepted of time as a means of unravelling, breaking up, this programmed brain. Once you see for yourself, clearly, absolutely, irrevocably, that time is not a freeing factor then already you begin to see cracks in the enclosure of the brain. Philosophers and scientists have said: time is a factor of growth, biologically, linguistically, technologically, but they have never enquired into the nature of psychological time. Any enquiry into psychological time implies the whole complex of psychological becoming — I am this, but I will be that; I am unhappy, unfulfilled, desperately lonely but tomorrow will be different. To perceive that time is the factor of conflict then that very perception is action; decision has taken place — *you* do not have to decide — the very perception is the action and decision.

There are multiple forms of conflict, there are thousands of opinions so there are thousands of forms of conflict. But we are not talking about the many forms of conflict but about conflict itself. We are not talking about your particular conflict — I don't get on with my wife, or in my business, or this or that — but the conflict of the human brain in its existence. Is there a perception — not born of memory, not born of knowledge — that sees the whole nature and structure of conflict; a perception of that whole? Is there such perception at all — not analytical perception, not intellectual observation of the various types of conflict, not an emotional response to conflict? Is there a perception not of remembrance, which is time, which is thought? Is there a perception which is not of time or thought, which can see the whole nature of conflict, and with that very perception bring about the ending of conflict? Thought is time. Thought is experience, knowledge, put together in the brain as memory. It is the result of time — 'I didn't know a week ago but I know now.' The multiplication of knowledge, the expansion of knowledge, the depth of knowledge, is of time. So thought is time — any psychological movement is time. If I want to go from here to Montreux, if I want to learn a language, if I want to meet somebody at a distant place, time is required. And that same outer process is carried on inwardly — 'I am not, I will be'. So thought is time. Thought and time are indivisible.

And we are asking the question: is there a perception which is not of time and thought — a perception that is entirely out of the pattern to which the brain has been accustomed? Is there such a thing that perhaps alone is going to solve the problem? We have not solved the problem in a million years of conflict; we are continuing the same pattern. We must find, intelligently, hesitantly, with care, if there is a way, if there is a perception which covers the whole of conflict, a perception which breaks the pattern.

35

The speaker has put this question forward. Now how shall we meet this together? He may be wrong, irrational, but after you have listened to him very carefully, it is your responsibility as well as the speaker's, to see if it is so, if it is possible. Do not say: 'Well it is not possible because I have not done it; it is not within my sphere; I have not thought enough about it; or, I do not want to think about it at all because I am satisfied with my conflict and because I am quite certain one day humanity will be free of conflict.' That is all just an escape from the problem. So are we together being aware of all the complexities of conflict, not denying it. It is there, it is there as actually as pain in the body. Are we aware without any choice that it is so and at the same time ask the question as to whether there is a different approach altogether?

Now, can we observe — it does not matter what it is — without the naming, without the remembrance? Look at your friend, or your wife, or whomever it is, observe that person without the words 'my wife' or 'my friend' or 'we belong to the same group' — without any of that — observe so that you are not observing through remembrance. Have you ever directly tried it? Look at the person without naming, without time and remembrance and also look at yourself — at the image that you have built about yourself, the image that you have built about the other; look as though you were looking for the first time — as you might at a rose for the first time. Learn to look; learn to observe this quality which comes without all the operation of thought. Do not say it is not possible. If you go to a professor, not knowing his subject but wanting to learn form him (I am not your professor), you go to listen. You do not say: 'I know something about it,' or 'You are wrong,' or 'You are right,' or 'I don't like your attitude.' You listen, you find out. As you begin to listen sensitively, with awareness, you begin to discover whether it is a phoney professor using a lot of words, or a professor who has really gone into the depths of his subject. Now, can we together so listen and observe, without the word, without remembrance, without all the movement of thought? Which means, complete attention; attention, not from a centre but attention which has no centre. If you have a centre from which you are attending, that is merely a form of concentration. But if you are attending and there is no centre, it means that you are giving complete attention; in that attention there is no time.

Many of you, fortunately or unfortunately, have heard the speaker for many years and one sees that this breaking of the 'programme' of the brain has not come about. You repeatedly listen to that statement year after year and it has not come about. Is it because you want to attain, to become, to have that state in which the pattern of the brain has been broken? You have listened, and it has not come about, and you are hoping that it will come about — which is another form of striving to become. So you are still in conflict. So you brush it all aside and say you will not come here any more because you have not got what you want — 'I want that but have not got it.' That wanting is the desire to be something and is a cause of conflict. That desire comes from the 'programmed' brain. We are saying: to break that programme, that pattern, observe without the movement of thought. It sounds very simple, but see the logic of it, the reason, the sanity, of it, not because the speaker says so, but because it is sane. Obviously one must exercise the capacity to be logical, rational and yet know its limitation; because rational, logical thinking is still part of thought. Knowing that thought is limited, be aware of that limitation and do not push it further because it will still be limited however far

37

you go, whereas if you observe a rose, a flower, without the word, without naming the colour, but just look at it, then that look brings about great sensitivity, breaks down this sense of heaviness of the brain, and gives extraordinary vitality. There is a totally different kind of energy when there is pure perception, which is not related to thought and time.

16th July, 1981

4

Order is necessary in our everyday activity; order in our action and order in our relationship with each other. One has to understand that the very quality of order is totally different from that of discipline. Order comes through directly learning about ourselves — not according to some philosopher or some psychologist. We discover order for ourselves when we are free from all sense of compulsion, from all sense of determined effort to obtain order along a particular path. That order comes very naturally. In that order there is righteousness. It is order, not according to some pattern, and not only in the outward world, which has become so utterly chaotic, but inwardly within ourselves where we are not clear, where we are confused and uncertain. Learning about ourselves is part of order. If you follow another, however erudite, you will not be able to understand yourself.

To find out what order is we must begin to understand the nature of our relationships. Our life is a movement in relationship; however much one may think one lives alone, one is always related to something or other, either to the past or to some projected image in the future. So, life is a movement in relationship and in that relationship there is disorder. We must examine closely why we live in such disorder in our relationships with each other — however intimate or superficial.

The speaker is not trying to persuade you to think in a particular direction, or put any kind of persuasive, subtle pressure on you. On the contrary, we are together thinking over our human problems and discovering what our relationship with each other is and whether in that relationship we can bring about order. To understand the full meaning of relationship with each other, however close, however distant, we must begin to understand why the brain creates images. We have images about ourselves and images about others. Why is it that each one has a peculiar image and identifies himself with that image? Is the image necessary, does it give one a sense of security? Does not the image bring about the separation of human beings?

We have to look closely at our relationship with wife, husband or friend; look very closely, not trying to avoid it, not trying to brush it aside. We must together examine and find out why human beings throughout the world have this extraordinary machinery that creates images, symbols, patterns. Is it because in those patterns, symbols and images, great security is found?

If you observe you will see that you have an image about yourself, either an image of conceit which is arrogant, or the contrary to that. Or you have accumulated a great deal of experience, acquired a great deal of knowledge, which in itself creates the image, the image of the expert. Why do we have images about ourselves? Those images separate people. If you have an image of yourself as Swiss or British or French and so on, that image not only distorts your observation of humanity but it also separates you from others. And wherever there is separation, division, there must be conflict — as there is conflict going on all over the world, the Arab against the Israeli, the Muslim against the Hindu, one Christian church against another. National division and economic division, all result from images, concepts, ideas and the brain clings

40

to these images — why? Is it because of our education, because of our culture in which the individual is most important and where the collective society is something totally different from the individual? That is part of our culture, part of our religious training and of our daily education. When one has an image about oneself as being British or American, that image gives one a certain security. That is fairly obvious. Having created the image about oneself that image becomes semi-permanent; behind that image, or in that image, one tries to find security, safety, a form of resistance. When one is related to another, however delicately, however subtly, psychically or physically, there is a response based on an image. If one is married or related intimately with somebody, an image is formed in one's daily life; whether one is acquainted for a week or ten years, the image is slowly formed about the other person step by step; every reaction is remembered, adding to the image and stored up in the brain so that the relationship — it may be physical, sexual, or psychical — is actually between two images, one's own and the other's.

The speaker is not saying something extravagant, or exotic, or fantastic, he is merely pointing out that these images exist. These images exist and one can never know another completely. If one is married or one has a girl friend, one can never know her completely; one thinks one knows her because having lived with that person one has accumulated memories of various incidents various irritations and all the occurrences which happen in daily life; and she also has experienced her reactions and their images are established in her brain. Those images play an extraordinarily important part in one's life. Apparently very few of us are free from any form of image. The freedom from images is real freedom. In that freedom there is no division brought about by images. If one is a

41

Hindu, born in India with all the conditioning to which one is subject, the conditioning of the race, or of a particular group with its superstitions, with its religious beliefs, dogmas, rituals — the whole structure of that society — one lives with that complex of images, which is one's conditioning. And however much one may talk about brotherhood, unity, wholeness, it is merely empty words having no actual daily meaning. But if one frees oneself from all that imposition, all the conditioning of all that superstitious nonsense, then one is breaking down the image. And also in one's relationship, if one is married or lives with somebody, is it possible not to create an image at all — not to record an incident which may be pleasurable or painful, in that particular relationship, not to record either the insult or the flattery, the encouragement or discouragement?

Is it possible not to record at all? Because if the brain is constantly recording everything that is happening, psychologically, then it is never free to be quiet, it can never be tranquil, peaceful. If the machinery of the brain is operating all the time it wears itself out. This is obvious. It is what happens in our relationships with each other — whatever the relationship is — and if there is constant recording of everything then the brain slowly begins to wither away and that is essentially old age.

So in investigating we come upon this question: is it possible in our relationships with all their reactions and subtleties, with all their essential responses, is there a possibility of not remembering? This remembering and recording is going on all the time. We are asking whether it is possible not to record psychologically, but only to record that which is absolutely necessary? In certain directions it is necessary to record. For example, one must record all that which is necessary to learn mathematics. If

I am to be an engineer I must record all the mathematics related to structures and so on. If I am to be a physicist I must record that which has already been established in that subject. To learn to drive a car I must record. But is it necessary in our relationships to record, psychologically, inwardly, at all? The remembrance of incidents past, is that love? When I say to my wife, 'I love you,' is that from a remembrance of all the things we have been through together — the incidents, the travail, the struggles, which are recorded, stored in the brain — is that remembrance actual love?

So is it possible to be free and not to record psychologically at all? It is only possible when there is complete attention. When there is complete attention there is no recording.

I do not know why we want explanations, or why it is that our brains are not swift enough to capture, to have an insight into, the whole thing immediately. Why is it that we cannot see this thing, the truth of all this, and let that truth operate and therefore cleanse the slate and have a brain that is not recording at all psychologically? But most human beings are rather sluggish, they rather like to live in their old patterns, in their particular habits of thought; anything new they reject because they think it is much better to live with the known rather than with the unknown. In the known there is safety — at least they think there is safety, security — so they keep on repeating, working and struggling within that field of the known. Can we observe without the whole process and machinery of memory operating?

What is love? This is a very complex question; all of us feel we love something or other, abstract love, love of a nation, love of a person, love of god, love of gardening, love of over-eating. We have abused the word love so greatly that we have to find out basically what love is.

43

Love is not an idea. Love of god is an idea, love of a symbol is still an idea. When you go to the church and kneel down and and pray, you are really worshipping, or praying to, something which thought has created. So, see what is happening, thought has created it — actually this is a fact — and you worship that which thought has created; which means you are worshipping, in a very subtle way, yourself. This may seem a sacrilegious statement, but it is a fact. That is what is happening throughout the world. Thought creates the symbol with all the attributes of that symbol, romantic or logical and sane; having created it you love it, you become totally intolerant of any other thing. All the gurus, all the priests, all the religious structures, are based on that. See the tragedy of it. Thought creates the flag, the symbol of a particular country, then you fight for it, you kill each other for it; your nation will destroy the earth in competition with another nation, and so the flag becomes a symbol of your love. We have lived for millions of years that way and we are still extraordinarily destructive, violent, brutal, cynical human beings.

When we say we love another, in that love there is desire, the pleasurable projections of the various activities of thought. One has to find out whether love is desire, whether love is pleasure, whether in love there is fear; for where there is fear there must be hatred, jealousy, anxiety, possessiveness, domination. There is beauty in relation-ship and the whole cosmos is a movement in relationship. Cosmos is order and when one has order in oneself one has order in one's relationships and therefore the possi-bility of order in our society. If one enquires into the nature of relationship one finds it is absolutely necessary to have order, and out of that order comes love. What is beauty? You see the fresh snow on the mountains this

44

morning, clean, a lovely sight. You see those solitary trees standing black against that white. Looking at the world about us you see the marvellous machinery, the extraordinary computer with its special beauty; you see the beauty of a face, the beauty of a painting, beauty of a poem — you seem to recognize beauty out there. In the museums or when you go to a concert and listen to Beethoven, or Mozart, there is great beauty — but always out there. In the hills, in the valleys with their running waters, and the flight of birds and the singing of a blackbird in the early morning, there is beauty. But is beauty only out there? Or is beauty something that only exists when the 'me' is not? When you look at those mountains on a sunny morning, sparkling clear against the blue sky, their very majesty drives away all the accumulated memories of yourself — for a moment. There the outward beauty, the outward magnificence, the majesty and the strength of the mountains, wipes away all your problems — if only for a second. You have forgotten yourself. When there is total absence of yourself beauty is. But we are not free of ourselves; we are selfish people, concerned with ourselves, with our importance or with our problems, with our agonies, sorrows and loneliness. Out of desperate loneliness we want identification with something or other and we cling to an idea, to a belief, to a person, especially to a person. In dependency all our problems arise. Where there is psychological dependency, fear begins. When you are tied to something corruption begins.

Desire is the most urgent and vital drive in our life. We are talking about desire itself, not desire for a particular thing. All religions have said that if you want to serve god you must subjugate desire, destroy desire, control desire. All the religions have said: substitute for desire an image

45

that thought has created — the image that the Christians have, that the Hindus have and so on. Substitute an image for the actual. The actual is desire — the burning of it and they think that one can overcome that desire by substituting something else for it. Or, surrender yourself to that which you think is the master, the saviour, the guru — which again is the activity of thought. This has been the pattern of all religious thinking. One has to understand the whole movement of desire; for obviously it is not love, nor yet compassion. Without love and compassion, meditation is utterly meaningless. Love and compassion have their own intelligence which is not the intelligence of cunning thought.

So it is important to understand the nature of desire, why it has played such an extraordinarily important part in our life; how it distorts clarity, how it prevents the extraordinary quality of love. It is important that we understand and do not suppress, do not try to control it or direct it in a particular direction, which you think may give you peace.

Please bear in mind that the speaker is not trying to impress you or guide and help you. But together we are walking a very subtle, complex path. We have to listen to each other to find out the truth about desire. When one understands the significance, the meaning, the fullness, the truth of desire, then desire has quite a different value or drive in one's life.

When one observes desire, is one observing it as an outsider looking at desire? Or is one observing desire as it arises? Not desire as something separate from oneself, one is desire. You see the difference? Either one observes desire, which one has when one sees something in the shop window which pleases one, and one has the desire to buy it so that the object is different from 'me', or else the desire is 'me', so there is a perception of desire without the observer watching desire.

One can look at a tree. 'Tree' is the word by which one recognizes that which is standing in the field. But one knows that the word 'tree' is not the tree. Similarly one's wife is not the word. But one has made the word one's wife. I do not know if you see all the subtleties of this. One must very clearly understand, from the beginning, that the word is not the thing. The word 'desire' is not the feeling of it — the extraordinary feeling there is behind that reaction. So one must be very watchful that one is not caught in the word. Also the brain must be active enough to see that the object may create desire — desire which is separate from the object. Is one aware that the word is not the thing and that desire is not separate from the observer who is watching desire? Is one aware that the object may create desire but the desire is independent of the object?

How does desire flower? Why is there such extra-ordinary energy behind it? If we do not understand deeply the nature of desire we will always be in conflict with each other. One may desire one thing and one's wife may desire another and the children may desire something different. So we are always at loggerheads with each other. And this battle, this struggle, is called love, relationship.

We are asking: what is the source of desire? We must be very truthful in this, very honest, for desire is very very deceptive, very subtle, unless we understand the root of it. For all of us sensory responses are important — sight, touch, taste, smell, hearing. And a particular sensory response may for some of us be more important than the other responses. If we are artistic we see things in a special way. If we are trained as an engineer then the sensory responses are different. so we never observe totally, with all the sensory responses. We each respond somewhat specially, divided. Is it possible to respond totally with all one's senses? See the importance of that. If one responds totally with all one's senses there is the elimination of the centralized observer. But when one responds to a particular thing in a special way then the division begins. Find out when you leave this tent, when you look at the flowing waters of the river, the light sparkling on the swiftness of the waters, find out if you can look at it with all your senses. Do not ask me how, for that becomes mechanical. But educate yourself in the understanding of total sensory response.

When you see something, the seeing brings about a response. You see a green shirt, or a green dress, the seeing awakens the response. Then contact takes place. Then from contact thought creates the image of you in that shirt or dress, then the desire arises. Or you see a car in the road, it has nice lines, it is highly polished and there is plenty of power behind it. Then you go around it, examine the engine. Then thought creates the image of you getting into the car and starting the engine, putting your foot down and driving it. So does desire begin and the source of desire is thought creating the image, up to that point there is no desire. There are the sensory responses, which are normal, but then thought creates the image and from that moment desire begins. Now, is it possible for thought not to arise and create the image? This is learning about desire, which in itself is discipline. Learning about desire is discipline, not the controlling of it. If you really learn about something it is finished. But if you say you must control desire, then you are in a totally different field altogether. When you see the whole of this movement you will find that thought with its image will not interfere; you will only see, have the sensation and what is wrong with that?

We are all so crazy about desire, we want to fulfil ourselves through desire. But we do not see what havoc it creates in the world — the desire for individual security, for individual attainment, success, power, prestige. We do not feel that we are totally responsible for everything we do. If one understands desire, the nature of it, then what place has it? Has it any place where there is love? Is love then something so extraordinarily outside of human existence that it has actually no value at all? Or, is it that we are not seeing the beauty and the depth, the greatness and sacredness of the actuality of it; is it that we have not the energy, the time to study, to educate ourselves, to understand what it is? Without love and compassion with its intelligence, meditation has very little meaning. Without that perfume that which is eternal can never be found. And that is why it is important to put the 'house' of our life, of our being, of our struggles, into complete order.

19th July, 1981

5

We have to consider together whether the brain, which is now only operating partially, has the capacity to function wholly, completely. Now we are only using a part of it, which one can observe for oneself. One can see that specialization, which may be necessary, brings about the functioning of only a part of the brain. If one is a scientist, specializing in that subject, naturally only one part of the brain is functioning; if one is a mathematician it is the same. In the modern world one has to specialize, and we are asking whether, even so, it is possible to allow the brain to operate wholly, completely.

And another question we are asking is: what is going to happen to humanity, to all of us, when the computer out-thinks man in accuracy and rapidity — as the computer experts are saying it will? With the development of the robot, man will only have, perhaps, two hours of work a day. This may be going to happen within the foreseeable future. Then what will man do? Is he going to be absorbed in the field of entertainment? That is already taking place: sports are becoming more important; there is the watching of television; and there are the varieties of religious entertainment. Or is he going to turn inwardly, which is not an entertainment but something which demands great capacity of observation, examination and non-personal perception? These are the two possibilities. The basic content of our human consciousness is the pursuit of pleasure and the avoidance of fear. Is humanity increasingly going to follow entertainment? One hopes these Gatherings are not a form of entertainment.

Now, can the brain be totally free so as to function wholly? — because any specialization, any following of a certain path, a certain groove, or pattern, inevitably implies that the brain is functioning partially and therefore with limited energy. We live in a society of specialization — engineers, physicists, surgeons, carpenters and the specializations of particular beliefs, dogmas and rituals. Certain specializations are necessary, such as that of the surgeon or carpenter, but in spite of that can the brain function completely, wholly, and therefore have tremendous energy? This is, I think, a very serious question into which we have to enquire together.

If one observes one's own activity one finds that the brain functions very partially, fragmentarily, with the result that one's energy becomes less and less as one grows older. Biologically, physically, when one is young one is full of vitality; but as one is educated, and then follows a livelihood that needs specialization, the activity of the brain becomes narrowed down, limited and its energy becomes less and less.

Though the brain may have to have a certain form of specialization — not necessarily religious specialization because that is superstition — as a surgeon for example, can it also operate wholly? It can only operate wholly, with all the tremendous vitality of a million years behind it, when it is completely free. Specialization, which is now necessary for a livelihood, may not be necessary if the computer takes over. It will not take over surgery, obviously. It will not take over the feeling of beauty, as when looking at the evening stars, but it may take over other functions altogether.

Can the human brain be totally free, without any form

51

of attachment — attachment to certain beliefs, experiences and so on? If the brain cannot be totally free it will deteriorate. When the brain is occupied with problems, with specialization, with a livelihood, it is in limited activity. But when the computer takes over, this activity will become less and less and therefore it will gradually deteriorate. This is not something in the future, it is actually happening now if one observes one's own mental activity.

Can your consciousness, with its basic content of fear, the pursuit of pleasure with all the implications of grief, pain and sorrow, being hurt inwardly and so on, become totally free? We may have other forms of consciousness, group consciousness, racial consciousness, national consciousness, the consciousness of the Catholic group, the Hindu group and so on but basically the content of our consciousness is fear, the pursuit of pleasure, with the resultant pain, sorrow and ultimately death. These comprise the central content of our consciousness. We are together observing the whole phenomenon of human existence, which is our existence. We are mankind, because our consciousness, whether as a Christian living in the Western world, or as a Muslim in the Middle East, or a Buddhist in the Asiatic world, is basically fear, the pursuit of pleasure and the never ending burden of pain, hurts, sorrow. One's consciousness is not personal to oneself. This is very difficult to accept because we have been so conditioned, so educated, that we resist the actual fact that we are not individuals at all, we are the whole of mankind. This is not a romantic idea, it is not a philosophical concept, it is absolutely not an ideal; examined closely, it is a fact. So we have to find out whether the brain can be free from the content of its consciousness.

Sirs, why do you listen to the speaker? Is it that in listening to the speaker you are listening to yourself? Is that what is taking place? The speaker is only pointing something out, acting as a mirror in which you see yourself, see the actuality of your own consciousness; it is not the description which the speaker is pointing out, which becomes merely an idea if you do no more than follow it. But if through the description, you yourself actually perceive your own state of mind, your own consciousness, then listening to the speaker has a certain importance. And if at the end of these talks you say to yourself: 'I have not changed; why? It is your fault. You have spoken for fifty years perhaps, and I have not changed', is it the fault of the speaker? Or you say: 'I have not been able to apply it; naturally it is the fault of the speaker'. Then you become cynical and do all kinds of absurd things. So please bear in mind that you are listening not so much to the speaker as looking at your own consciousness through the description in words — which is the consciousness of all humanity. The Western world may believe in certain religious symbols and certain rituals; the Eastern world does likewise, but behind it all there is the same fear, the same pursuit of pleasure, the same burden of greed, pain, of being hurt and wanting to achieve — all of which is common to the whole of humanity.

So, in listening we are learning about ourselves, not just following the description. We are actually learning to look at ourselves and therefore bringing about a total freedom in which the whole of the brain can operate. After all, meditation, love and compassion are the operation of the whole of the brain. When there is the operation of the whole there is integral order. When there is integral, inward order, there is total freedom. It is only then that there can be something which is timelessly sacred. That is not a reward; that is not something to be achieved; that which is eternally timeless, sacred, comes about only when the brain is totally free to function in wholeness.

The content of our consciousness is put together by all the activities of thought; can that content ever be freed so that there is a totally different dimension altogether? So let us observe the whole movement of pleasure. There is not only biological, including sexual, pleasure, there is also pleasure in possessions, pleasure in having money, pleasure in achieving something that you have been working towards; there is pleasure in power, political or religious, in power over a person; there is pleasure in the acquisition of knowledge, and in the expression of that knowledge as a professor, as a writer, as a poet; there is the gratification that comes about through leading a very strict, moral and ascetic life, the pleasure of achieving something inwardly which is not common to ordinary man. This has been the pattern of our existence for millions of years. The brain has been conditioned to it and therefore has become limited. Anything that is conditioned must be limited and therefore the brain, when it is pursuing the many forms of pleasure, must inevitably become small, limited, narrow. And probably, unconsciously realising this, one seeks different forms of entertainment, a release through sex, through different kinds of fulfilment. Please observe it in yourself, in your own activity in daily life. If you observe, you will see that one's brain is occupied all day with something or other, chattering, talking endlessly, going on like a machine that never stops. And in this way the brain is gradually wearing itself out — and it is going to become inactive if the computer takes its place.

So, why are human beings caught in this perpetual

persuit of pleasure — why? Is it because they are so utterly lonely? Are they escaping from that sense of isolation? Is it that they have been, from childhood, conditioned to this? Is it because thought creates the image of pleasure and then pursues it? Is thought the source of pleasure? For example, one has had some kind of pleasure, eating very tasty food, or sexual pleasure, or the pleasure of being flattered and the brain registers that pleasure. The incidents which have brought about pleasure have been recorded in the brain, and the remembrance of these incidents of yesterday, or last week, is the movement of thought. Thought is the movement of pleasure; the brain has registered incidents, pleasurable and exciting, worth remembering, and thought projects them into the future and pursues them. So the question then is: why does thought carry on the memory of an incident that is over and finished? Is not that part of our occupation? A man who wants money, power, position, is perpetually occupied with it. Perhaps, the brain is similarly occupied with the remembrance of something of a week ago which gave great pleasure, being held in the brain, which thought projects as future pleasure and pursues. The repetition of pleasure is the movement of thought and therefore limited; therefore the brain can never function wholly, it can only function partially.

Now the next question that arises is: if this is the pattern of thought, how can thought be stopped, or rather, how can the brain stop registering the incident of yesterday which gave delight? That is the obvious question, but why does one put it? Why? Is it because one wants to escape from the movement of pleasure, and that that very escape is yet another form of pleasure? Whereas if you see the fact that the incident which gave great delight, pleasure, excitement, is over, that it is no longer a living thing, but something which happened a week ago — it was a living thing then but it is not so now — can you not finish with it, end it, not carry it over? It is not *how* to end it or *how* to stop it. It is just to see factually how the brain, how thought, is operating. If one is aware of that, then thought itself will come to an end. The registering of pleasure is ended, finished.

Fear is the common state of all mankind, whether you live in a small house or in a palace, whether you have no work or plenty of work, whether you have tremendous knowledge about everything on earth or are ignorant, or whether you are a priest or the highest representative of god, or whatever, there is still this deep rooted fear which is common to all mankind. That is a common ground on which all humanity stands. There is no question about it. It is an absolute, irrevocable fact, it cannot be contradicted. As long as the brain is caught in this pattern of fear its operation is limited and therefore can never function wholly. So it is necessary, if humanity is to survive completely as human beings and not as machines, to find out for oneself whether it is possible to be totally free from fear.

We are concerned with fear itself, not with the expressions of fear. What is fear? When there is fear, is there at that very moment a recognition as fear? Is that fear describable at the moment the reaction is taking place? Or does the description come after? 'After' is time. Suppose one is afraid: either one is afraid of something, afraid of something that one has done in the past which one does not want another to know, or something has happened in the past which again awakens fear, or is there a fear by itself without an object? At the second when there is fear does one call it fear? Or does that happen only afterwards? Surely it is after it has happened.

56

Which means that previous incidents of fear which have been held in the brain are remembered immediately after the reaction takes place; the memory says 'That is fear'. At the immediacy of the reaction one does not call it fear. It is only after it has happened that one names it as fear. The naming of it as fear is from the remembrance of other incidents that have arisen which have been named fear. One remembers those fears of the past and the new reaction arises which one immediately identifies with the word fear. That is simple enough. So there is always the memory operating on the present.

So; is fear time? — the fear of something which happened a week ago, which has caused that feeling which we have named as fear and the future implication that it must not happen again; yet it might happen again, therefore one is afraid of it. So one asks oneself: is it time that is the root of fear?

So what is time? Time by the watch is very simple. The sun rises at a certain time and sets at a certain time — yesterday, today and tomorrow. That is a natural sequence of time. There is also psychological, inward time. The incident which happened last week, which has given pleasure, or which awakened the sense of fear, is remembered and projected into the future — I may lose my position, I may lose my money, I may lose my wife — time. So is fear part of psychological time? It looks like it. And what is psychological time? Not only does physical time need space, but psychological time needs space also — yesterday, last week, modified today, tomorrow. There is space and time. That is simple. So, is fear the movement of time? And is not the movement of time, psychologically, the movement of thought? So thought is time and time is fear — obviously. One has had pain sitting with the dentist. It is stored, remembered, projected; one hopes not to have that pain again — thought is moving. So fear is a movement of thought in space and time. If one sees that, not as an idea, but as an actuality (which means one has to give to that fear complete attention at the moment it arises) then it is not registered. Do this and you will find out for yourself. When you give complete attention to an insult, there is no insult. Or if somebody comes along and says, 'What a marvellous person you are' and you pay attention it is like water off a duck's back. The movement of fear is thought in time and space. That is a fact. It is not something described by the speaker. If you have observed it for yourself, then it is an absolute fact, you cannot escape from it. You cannot escape from a fact, it is always there. You may try to avoid it, you may try to suppress it, try every kind of escape, but it is always there. If you give complete attention to the fact that fear is the movement of thought, then fear is not, psychologically. The content of our consciousness is the movement of thought in time and space. Whether that thought is very limited, or wide and extensive, it is still a movement in time and space.

Thought has created many different forms of power in ourselves, psychologically, but they are all limited. When there is freedom from limitation there is an astonishing sense of power, not mechanical power but a tremendous sense of energy. It has nothing to do with thought and therefore that power, that energy cannot be misused. But if thought says, 'I will use it', then that power, that energy, is dissipated.

Another factor which exists in our consciousness is sorrow, grief, pain and the wounds and hurts that remain in most human beings from childhood. That psychological hurt, the pain of it, is remembered, it is held on to; grief arises from it; sorrow is involved in it. There is the global sorrow of mankind which has faced thousands and thousands of wars, for which millions of people have cried. The war machine is still with us, directed by politicians, reinforced by our nationalism, by our feeling that we are separate from the rest, 'we' and 'they', 'you' and 'me'. It is a global sorrow which the politicians are building, building, building. We are ready for another war and when we prepare for something there must be some kind of explosion somewhere — it may not be in the Middle East, it may happen here. As long as we are preparing for something we are going to get it — it is like preparing food. But we are so stupid that all this goes on — including terrorism.

We are asking whether this whole pattern of being hurt, knowing loneliness and pain, resisting, withdrawing, isolating ourselves, which causes further pain, can come to an end; whether the grief, the sorrow of losing some precious belief that we have held, or the disillusionment that comes when we lose somebody we have followed, for whom we have struggled, surrendered ourselves, can also come to an end? Is it possible *ever* to be free of all this? It is possible if we apply ourselves, not just endlessly talk about it. As it is we realize that we are hurt psychologically from childhood, we see all the consequences of that hurt, which we resist, from which we withdraw, not wanting to be hurt any more. We encourage isolation and therefore build a wall round ourselves. In our relationships we are doing the same thing.

The consequences of being hurt from childhood are pain, resistance, withdrawal, isolation, deeper and deeper fear. And, as the speaker has said, there is the global sorrow of mankind; human beings have been tortured through wars, tortured under dictatorships, totalitarianism, tortured in different parts of the world. And there is the sorrow of my brother, son, wife, running away, or dying; the sorrow of separation, the sorrow that comes about when one is deeply interested in something and the other is not. In all this sorrow there is no compassion, there is no love. The ending of sorrow brings love — not pleasure, not desire, but love. Where there is love there is compassion with which comes intelligence, which has nothing whatever to do with the 'intelligence' of thought.

We have to look very closely at ourselves as humanity, at why we have borne all these things all our lives, at why we have never ended this condition. Is it part indolence, part habit? We generally say: 'It is part of our habit, part of our conditioning. What am I to do about it? How am I to uncondition myself? I cannot find the answer; I will go to the guru next door' — or further away, or the priest, or this or that. We never say: 'Let us look at ourselves closely and see if we can break through it, like any other habit.' The habit of smoking can be broken, or that of drugs and alcohol. But we say: 'What does it matter. I am getting old anyhow, the body is destroying itself, so what does little more pleasure matter?' So do we carry on. We do not feel utterly responsible for all the things we do. We either blame it on the environment, on society, on our parents, on past hereditary; we find some excuse but never apply ourselves. If we really have the urge, the immediate urge, to find out why we are hurt, it can be done. We are hurt because we have built an image about ourselves. That is a fact. When one says, 'I am hurt', it is the image that one has about oneself that is hurt. Somebody comes along and puts his heavy boot on that image and one gets hurt. One gets hurt through comparison: 'I am this but somebody else is better'. As long as one has an image about oneself one is going to get hurt. That is a fact and if one does not pay attention to that fact, but retains an image of oneself of any kind somebody is going to put a pin into it and one is going to get hurt. If one has an image about oneself as addressing large audiences and being famous, having gained a reputation which one wants to maintain, then someone is going to hurt it — somebody else with a bigger audience. If one gives complete attention to the image one has about oneself — attention, not concentration but attention — then one will see that the image has no meaning and it disappears.

21st July, 1981

6

I think we ought to talk over together, going into it rather
deeply, the implication of sorrow, so as to find out for
ourselves whether sorrow and love can exist together.
And also what is our relationship to the sorrow of
mankind? — not only to our own personal daily grief,
hurt, pain, and the sorrow that comes with death.
Mankind has suffered thousands of wars; there seems to
be no end to wars. We have left it to the politicians, all
over the world, to bring about peace, but what they are
doing, if you have understood them, will never bring
peace. We are all preparing for war. The preparations are
going to have some kind of blow up somewhere in the
world. We human beings have never been able to live in
peace with each other. We talk about it a great deal. The
religions have preached peace — peace on earth and
goodwill — but apparently it has never been possible to
have peace on earth, on the earth on which we live, which
is not the British earth or the French earth, it is our earth.
We have never been able to resolve the problem of killing
each other.

Probably we have violence in our hearts. We have
never been free from a sense of antagonism, a sense of
retaliation, never free from our fears, sorrows, wounds
and the pain of daily existence; we never have peace and
comfort, we are always in travail. That is part of our life,
part of our daily suffering. Man has tried many many ways
to be free of this suffering without love; he has suppressed

62

it, escaped from it, identified himself with something greater, handed himself over to some ideal, or belief or faith. Apparently this sorrow can never end; we have become accustomed to it, we put up with it, we tolerate it and we never ask ourselves seriously, with a great sense of awareness, whether it is possible to end it.

We should also talk over together the immense implications of death. Death is part of life, though we generally postpone or avoid even talking about it. It is there and we ought to go into it. And we should also enquire whether love — not the remembrance of pleasure which has nothing to do with love and compassion — whether love with its own peculiar all-comprehending intelligence can exist in our life.

First of all: do we, as human beings, want to be really free from sorrow? Have we ever actually gone into it, faced it and understood all the movement of it, the implications involved in it? Why is it that we human beings — who are so extraordinarily clever in the technological world — have never resolved the problem of sorrow? It is important to talk this question over together, and find out for ourselves whether sorrow can really end.

We all suffer in various ways. There is the sorrow for death of someone, there is the sorrow of great poverty — which the East knows very well — and the great sorrow of ignorance — 'ignorance' not in the sense of book knowledge but the ignorance of not knowing oneself totally, the whole complex activity of the self. If we do not understand that very deeply then there remains the sorrow of that ignorance. There is the sorrow of never being able to realise something fundamentally, deeply — though we are very clever at achieving technological success and other successes in this world. We haver never been able to understand pain, not only physical pain, but the deep psychological pain, however learned or not very erudite we may be. There is the sorrow of constant struggle, the conflict from the moment we are born until we die. There is the personal sorrow of not being beautiful outwardly or inwardly. There is the sorrow of attachment with its fear, with its corruption. There is the sorrow of not being loved and craving to be loved. There is the sorrow of never realising something beyond thought, something which is eternal. And ultimately there is the sorrow of death.

We have described various forms of sorrow. The basic factor of sorrow is self-centred activity. We are all so concerned with ourselves, with our endless problems, with old age, with not being able to have a deep inward yet global outlook. We all have images of ourselves and of others. The brain is always active in day dreaming, being occupied with something or other, or creating pictures and ideas from the imagination. From childhood one gradually builds the structure of the image which is 'me'. Each one of us is doing this constantly; it is that image, which is 'me', that gets hurt. When the 'me' is hurt there is resistance, the building of a wall round oneself so as not to be hurt any more; and this creates more fear and isolation, the feeling of having no relationship, the encouraging of loneliness which also brings about sorrow.

After having described the various forms of sorrow, can we look at it without verbalization, without running away from it into intellectual adaptation to some form of religious or intellectual conclusion? Can we look at it completely, not moving away from it, but staying with it? Suppose I have a son who is deaf or blind; I am responsible, and it gives sorrow knowing that he can never look at the beautiful sky, never hear the running waters. There is this sorrow: remain with it, do not move away from it. Or suppose I have great sorrow for the death of someone with whom I have lived for many years. Then there is this sorrow which is the essence of isolation; we feel totally isolated, completely alone. Now, remain completely with that feeling, not verbalizing it, not rationalizing it, or escaping from it, or trying to transcend it — all of which is the movement that thought brings about. When there is that sorrow and thought does not enter into it at all — which means that you are completely sorrow, not trying to overcome sorrow, but totally sorrow — then there is the disappearance of it. It is only when there is the fragmentation of thought that there is travail.

When there is sorrow, remain with it without a single movement of thought so that there is the wholeness of it. The wholeness of sorrow is not that I am in sorrow, I am sorrow — and then there is no fragmentation involved in it. When there is that totality of sorrow, no movement away from it, then there is the withering away of it.

Without ending sorrow how can there be love? Strangely we have associated sorrow and love. I love my son and when he dies I am full of sorrow — sorrow we associate with love. Now we are asking: when there is suffering can love exist at all? But is love desire? Is love pleasure — so that when that desire, that pleasure, is denied, there is suffering? We say that suffering as jealousy, attachment, possession, is all part of love. That is our conditioning, that is how we are educated, that is part of our inheritance, tradition. Now, love and sorrow cannot possibly go together. That is not a dogmatic statement, or a rhetorical assertion. When one looks into the depth of sorrow and understands the movement of it in which is involved pleasure, desire, attachment, and the consequences of that attachment, which bring about corruption, when one is aware without any choice, without any movement, aware of the whole nature of sorrow, then can love exist with sorrow? Or is love something entirely different? We ought to be clear that devotion to a person, to a symbol, to the family, is not love. If I am devoted to you for various reasons, there is a motive behind that devotion. Love has no motive. If there is a motive it is not love, obviously. If you give me pleasure, sexually, or various forms of comfort, then there is dependency; the motive is my dependence on you because you give me something in return; and as we live together I call that love. Is it? So one questions the whole thing and asks oneself: where there is motive can love exist?

Where there is ambition, whether in the physical world, or in the psychological world — ambition to be on top of everything, to be a great success, to have power, religiously, or physically — can love exist? Obviously not. We recognise that it cannot exist and yet we go on. Look what happens to the brain when we play such tricks. I am ambitious, I want to be spiritually next to god, specially on his right hand; I want to achieve illumination — you know, all that deception; you cannot achieve illumination; you cannot possibly achieve that which is beyond time. Competitiveness, conformity, jealousy, fearfulness, hate, all that is going on, psychologically, inwardly. We are either conscious of it, or we deliberately avoid it. Yet I say to my wife or father, whoever it is, 'I love you.' What happens when there is such deep contradiction in my life, in my relationship? How can that contradiction have any sense of deep integrity? And yet that is what we are doing until we die, can one live in this world without ambition, without competitiveness? Look at what is happening in the outward world. There is competition between various

66

nations; the politicians are competing with each other, economically, technologically, in building up the instruments of war; and so we are destroying ourselves. We allow this to go on because we are also inwardly competitive.

As we pointed out, if a few really understand what we have been talking about for the last fifty years, and are really deeply involved and have brought about the end of fear, sorrow and so on, then that will affect the whole of the consciousness of mankind. Perhaps you are doubtful whether it will affect the consciousness of mankind? Hitler and his kind have affected the consciousness of mankind — Napoleon, the Caesars, the butchers of the world have affected mankind. Also the good people have affected mankind — I do not mean respectable people. The good are those who live life wholly, not fragmented. The great teachers of the world have affected human consciousness. But if there was a group of people who had understood what we have been talking about — not verbally but actually living life with great integrity — then it would affect the whole consciousness of man. This is not a theory. This is an actual fact. If you understand that simple fact you will see that it goes right through; television, newspapers, everything, is affecting the consciousness of man. So love cannot exist where there is a motive, where there is attachment, where there is ambition and competitiveness, love is not desire and pleasure. Just feel that, see it.

We are going into all this so as to bring about order in our life — order in our 'house', which has no order. There is so much disorder in our life and without establishing an order that is whole, integral, meditation has no meaning whatsoever. If one's 'house' is not in order one may sit in meditation, hoping that through that meditation one will bring about order; but what happens when one is living in disorder and one meditates? One has fanciful dreams, illusions and all kinds of nonsensical results. But a sane, intelligent, logical man, must first establish order in daily life, then he can go into the depths of meditation, into the meaning and the beauty of it, the greatness of it, the worth of it.

Whether we are very young, middle aged or old, death is part of our life, just as love, pain, suspicion, arrogance, are all part of life. But we do not see death as part of our life; we want to postpone it, or put it as far away from us as possible, so we have a time interval between life and death. What is death? This question is again rather complex.

The Christian concept of death and suffering and the Asiatic conclusion about reincarnation are just beliefs and like all beliefs they have no substance. So put those aside and let us go into it together. It may be unpleasant; you may not want to face it. You are living now, healthily, having pleasure, fear, anxiety and tomorrow there is hope and you do not want to be concerned with the ending of all this. But if we are intelligent, sane, rational, we have to face not only the living and all the implications of the living, but also the implications of dying. We must know both. That is the wholeness of life in which there is no division. So what is death apart from the physical ending of an organism that has lived wrongly, addicted to drink, to drugs and over indulgence or asceticism and denial? The body goes through this constant battle between the opposites, it has not a balanced harmonious life, but one of extremes. Also the body goes through great stress imposed by thought. Thought dictates and the body is controlled thereby; and thought being limited brings about disharmony. It causes us to live in disharmony physically, forcing, controlling, subjugating, driving the body — this is what we are all doing including fasting for political or religious reasons, which is violence. The body may endure all this for many years, reaching old age and not getting senile. But the body will inevitably come to an end, the organism will die; is that what death is? Is the coming to an end of the organism, either through some disease, old age or accident, what we are concerned about? Is it that thought identifies itself with the body, with the name, with the form, with all the memories, and says, 'Death must be avoided'? Is it that we are afraid of the coming to an end of a body that has been looked after, cared for? Perhaps we are not afraid of that especially, perhaps slyly anxious about it, but that is not of great importance. What is far more important for us is the ending of the relationships that we have had, the pleasures that we have had, the memories, pleasant and unpleasant, all of which make up what we call living — the daily living, going to the office, the factory, doing some skillful job, having a family, being attached to the family, with all the memories of that family, my son, my daughter, my wife, my husband, in the family unit — which is fast disappearing. There is the feeling of being related to somebody, though in that relationship there may be great pain and anxiety; the feeling of being at home with somebody; or not at home with anybody. Is that what we are afraid of? — the ending of my relationships, my attachments, the ending of something I have known, something to which I have clung, something in which I have specialized all my life, — am I afraid of the ending of all that? That is the ending of all that is 'me' — the family, the name, the home, the tradition, the inheritance, the cultural education and racial inheritance, all that is 'me', the 'me' that is struggling or that is happy. Is that what we are afraid of? — the ending of 'me', which is the ending, psychologically, of the life which I am leading, the life which I know with its pain and sorrow. Is that what we are afraid of?

69

If we are afraid of that and have not resolved that fear, still death inevitably comes, then what happens to that consciousness, which is not your consciousness but the consciousness of mankind, the consciousness of the vast whole of humanity? As long as I am afraid as an individual with my limited consciousness, it is that that I am afraid of. It is that of which I am scared. One realises that it is not a fact that one's consciousness is totally separate from that of everybody else — one sees that separateness is an illusion, it is illogical, unhealthy. So one realises, perhaps in one's heart, in one's feeling, that one is the whole of mankind — not an individual consciousness, which has no meaning. And one has lived this kind of life, which is pain, sorrow, anxiety, and if one's brain has not transformed some of all that, one's life is only a further confusion to the wholeness. But if one realises that one's consciousness is the consciousness of mankind, and that for the human consciousness one is totally responsible, then freedom from the limitation of that consciousness becomes extraordinarily important. When there is that freedom then one is contributing to the breaking down of the limitation of that consciousness. Then death has a totally different meaning.

One has lived a so-called individual life, concerned about oneself and one's problems. Those problems never end, they increase. One has lived that kind of life. One has been brought up, educated, conditioned, to that kind of life. You come along as a friend — you like me, or you love me — you say to me: 'Look, your consciousness is not yours; you suffer as other people suffer'. I listen to it and I do not reject what you say, for it makes sense, it is sane and I see that in what you have told me there can perhaps be peace in the world. And I say to myself: 'Now, can I be free from fear?' I see that I am responsible, totally, for the whole of consciousness. I

70

see that when I am investigating fear I am helping the total human consciousness to lessen fear. Then death has a totally different meaning. I no longer have phantasies that I am going to sit next to god, or that I am going to heaven through some peculiar nebula. I am living a life which is not my particular life. I am living a life of the whole of humanity and if I understand death, if I understand grief, I am cleansing the whole of the consciousness of mankind. That is why it is important to understand the meaning of death and perhaps to find that death has great significance, great relationship with love, because where you end something love is. When you end attachment completely then love is.

23rd July, 1981

7

We have talked about the complex problem of existence, about the forming of images in our relationships with each other and the images which thought projects and which we worship. We have talked about fear, pleasure and the ending of sorrow and the question of what love is, apart from all the travail that is involved in so-called love. We have talked about compassion with its intelligence and about death. We ought now to talk about religion.

Many intellectuals, throughout the world, shy away from the subject of religion. They see what religions are in the present world, with their beliefs, dogmas, rituals and the hierarchical set-up of their established existence; and they rather scoff at and run away from anything to do with religion. And as they age and come near to that threshold called death, they often revert to their old conditioning: they become Catholics or pursue some guru in India or Japan. Religion throughout the world has lost its credibility and no longer has any significance in daily life. The more you examine, the more you are aware of the whole content of all the religious structures, the more sceptical you become about the whole business and like the intellectuals, you have nothing to do with them. And those who are not sceptical, treat religions romantically, emotionally, or as a form of entertainment.

If one puts aside the intellectual, the romantic and sentimental attitudes towards religions, one can then begin to ask, not with any naivety, but with seriousness:

what is religion? — not looking for the mere meaning of that word, but deeply. Man, from ancient times, has always thought that there must be something beyond ordinary daily life, the ordinary misery, confusion and conflict of daily life. In his search he has invented all kinds of philosophies, created all kinds of images — from those of the ancient Egyptians and the ancient Hindus to modern times — always getting caught apparently in some kind of delusion. He deludes himself and out of those delusions he creates all kinds of activities. If one could brush all that aside, not hypnotising oneself, being free from illusion, then one can begin to examine, enquire very profoundly if there is something beyond all the contagion of thought, all the corruption of time, if there is something beyond one's usual existence in space and time and if there is any path to it, or no path, and how the mind can reach it, or come to it. If one asks that of oneself then how shall one set about it? Is any kind of preparation necessary — discipline, sacrifice, control, a certain period of preparation and then advance?

First of all it is important to understand that one should be free of all illusions. So, what creates illusions? Is it not the desire to reach something, to experience something out of the ordinary — extrasensory perception, visions, spiritual experiences? One must be very clear as to the nature of desire and understand the movement of desire, which is thought with its image and also have no motive in one's enquiry. It may seem very difficult to have no intention, to have no sense of direction so that the brain is free to enquire. There must be order in one's house, in one's existence, in one's relationships, in one's activity. Without order, which is freedom, there can be no virtue. Virtue, righteousness, is not something that is intellectually cultivated. Where there is order there is virtue; that order is something that is living, not a routine, a habit.

Secondly: is there something to be learnt? Is there something to be learnt from another? One can learn from another, history, biology, mathematics, physics; the whole complex knowledge of the technological world one can learn from another, from books. Is there something to be learned from psychology about our lives, about that which is eternal? — if there is something eternal. Or is it that there is nothing to learn from another because all the human experience, all the psychological knowledge that humanity has gathered together for millions of years, is within oneself. If that is so, if one's consciousness is that of the whole of mankind then it seems rather absurd, rather naive, to try to learn from somebody else about oneself. It requires complete clarity of observation to learn about ourselves. That is simple. So there is no psychological authority and no spiritual authority, because the whole history of mankind, which is the story of humanity, is in oneself. Therefore there is nothing to experience. There is nothing to be learnt from somebody who says: 'I know' or, 'I will show you the path to truth' — from the priests throughout the world, the interpreters between the highest and the lowest. To learn about, to understand, oneself, all authority must be set aside. Obviously. Authority is part of oneself; one is the priest, the disciple, the teacher, one is the experience and one is the ultimate — if one knows how to understand.

There is nothing to be learnt from anybody, including the speaker; especially one must not be influenced by the speaker. One has to be free to enquire very, very deeply, not superficially. One may have done all the superficial enquiry during the last five or fifty years, and have come to the point when one has established order, more or less, in one's life, and as one goes along one may establish

74

greater order, so that one can ask: what is the religious mind which can understand what meditation is?

Within the last fifteen years, that word meditation has become very popular in the West. Before that, only very few, who had been to Asia, enquired into the Eastern forms of meditation. The Asiatics have said that only through meditation can you come to, or understand, that which is the timeless, which has no measure. But during recent years, those who have nothing to do but call themselves gurus, have come over to the West bringing that word. It has become a word that has made meditation seem like a drug. There are also the various systems of meditation — the Tibetan, the Hindu, the Japanese Zen, and so on. These systems have been invented by thought and thought being limited the systems must inevitably be limited. And also they become mechanical, for if you repeat, repeat, your mind naturally goes dull, rather stupid and utterly gullible. It is common sense all this, but there is such eagerness to experience something spiritual, either through drugs, through alcohol, or by following a system of meditation which it is hoped will give some kind of exciting experience; there is such boredom with the daily life of going to the office for the next forty years and at the end of it to die. There is such boredom with the established religions that when somebody comes along with some fantastic notions people fall for them. This is happening; this is not exaggeration, this is not attacking anybody personally but a statement of the nonsense that is going on.

So, if one is sufficiently aware of all this one will have put it aside, for it is utterly meaningless; one does not have to go to India, or Tibet, or to Rome, if one uses common sense and has a critical mind that is questioning what others say and also questioning oneself. It is important to question anything that one considers to be correct, noble, or a real experience and it is essential to maintain a mind that is capable, rational, sane, free from all the illusions and any form of self-hypnosis.

Then what is a human being? The human being has lived on thought; all the architecture, all the music, the things that are inside the churches, the temples and mosques, they are all invented by thought. All our relationships are based on thought, though we say, 'I love you', it is still based on the image which thought has created about another. Thought, to the human being, is astonishingly important; and thought itself is limited; its action is to bring about fragmentation — the fragmentation between people — my religion, my country, my god, my belief as opposed to yours, all that is the movement of thought, space and time.

Meditation is the capacity of the brain which is no longer functioning partially — the brain which has freed itself from its conditioning and is therefore functioning as a whole. The meditation of such a brain is different from the mere contemplation of one conditioned as a Christian or a Hindu, whose contemplation is from a background, from a conditioned mind. Comtemplation does not free one from conditioning. Meditation demands a great deal of enquiry and becomes extraordinarily serious in order not to function partially. By partially is meant to function in a particular specialization or particular occupation that makes the brain narrow in accepting beliefs, traditions, dogmas and rituals, all of which are invented by thought. The Christians use the word 'faith' — faith in god, in providence so that things will come out all right. The Asiatics have their own forms of faith — karma, reincarnation and spiritual evolution. Meditation is different from contemplation in the sense that meditation demands that the brain acts wholly and is no longer conditioned to act partially. That is the requirement for meditation, otherwise it has no meaning.

So the question is: is it possible to live in this world, which demands certain forms of specialization, a skillful mechanic, mathematician, or housewife, yet to be free from specialization? Suppose I am a theoretical physicist and have spent most of my life in mathematical formulation, thinking about it, questioning it, cultivating considerable knowledge about it, so that my brain has become specialized, narrowed down and then I begin to enquire into meditation. Then in my enquiry into meditation I can only partially understand the significance and the depth of it because I am anchored in something else, in the theoretical physics of my profession; anchored there I begin to enquire theoretically whether there is meditation whether there is the timeless; so my enquiry becomes partial again. But I have to live in this world; I am a professor at a university; I have a wife and children, I have that responsibility and perhaps I am also ill; yet I want to enquire very profoundly into the nature of truth, which is part of meditation. So the question is: is it possible to be specialized as a theoretical physicist and yet leave it at a certain level so that my brain (the brain which is the common brain of all humanity) can say: yes, it has that specialized function but that function is not going to interfere?

If I am a carpenter, I know the quality of the wood, the grain, the beauty of the wood and the tools with which to work it. And I see that that is natural and I also see that the brain that has cultivated the speciality cannot possibly understand the wholeness of meditation. If as a carpenter I understand this, the truth of it, that I, as a carpenter have a place, but also that that specialization has no place in the wholeness of comprehension, in the wholeness of understanding meditation, then that specialization becomes a small affair.

So then we begin to ask: what is meditation? First of all, meditation demands attention, which is to give your whole capacity, energy, in observation. Attention is different from concentration. Concentration is an effort made by thought to focus its capacity, its energy, on a particular subject. When you are in school you are trained to concentrate, that is to bring all your energy to a particular point. In concentration you are not allowing any other kind of thoughts to interfere; concentration implies the controlling of thought, not allowing it to wander away but keeping it focused on a particular subject. It is the operation of thought which focuses attention, focuses energy, on that subject. In that operation of thought there is compulsion, control. So in concentration there is the controller and the controlled. Thought is wandering off; thought says it should not wander off, and I bring it back as the controller who says, 'I must concentrate on this.' So there is a controller and the controlled. Who is the controller? The controller is part of thought and the controller is the past. The controller says, 'I have learnt a great deal and it is important for me, the controller, to control thought.' That is: thought has divided itself as the controller and the controlled; it is a trick that thought is playing upon itself. Now, in attention there is no controller, nor is there the controlled, there is only attention. So a careful examination is required into the nature of concentration with its controller and the controlled. All our life there is this controller — 'I must do this, I must not do that, I must control my desires, control my anger, control my impetus.'

We must be very clear in understanding what concentration is and what attention is. In attention there is no controller. So, is there in daily existence, a way of living in which every form of psychological control ceases to exist? — because control means effort, it means division between the controller and the controlled; I am angry, I must control my anger; I smoke, I must not smoke and I must resist smoking. We are saying there is something totally different and this may be misunderstood and may be rejected altogether because it is very common to say that all life is control — if you do not control you will become permissive, nonsensical, without meaning, therefore you must control. Religions, philosophies, teachers, your family, your mother, they all encourage you to control. We have never asked: who is the controller? The controller is put together in the past, the past which is knowledge, which is thought. Thought has separated itself as the controller and the controlled. Concentration is the operation of that. Understanding that, we are asking a much more fundamental question, which is: can one live in this world, with a family and responsibilities, without a shadow of control?

See the beauty of that question. Our brain has been trained for thousands of years to inhibit, to control, and now it is never operating with the wholeness of itself. See for yourself what it is doing; watch your own brain in operation, rationally, critically examining it in a way in which there is no deception or hypnosis. Most of the meditations that have been put forward from the Asiatic world involve control; control thought so that you have a mind that is at peace, that is quiet, that is not eternally chattering. Silence, quietness and the absolute stillness of the mind, the brain, are necessary in order to perceive and to achieve this these forms of meditation, however subtle, have control as their basis. Alternatively you hand yourself over to a guru, or to some ideal and you can forget yourself because you have given yourself over to something and therefore you are at peace, but again it is the movement of thought, desire and the excitement of attaining something you have been offered.

Attention is not the opposite of concentration. The opposite has its root in its own opposite. If love is the opposite of hate, then love is born out of hate. Attention is not the opposite of concentration, it is totally divorced from it. Does attention need effort? That is one of our principal activities; I must make an effort; I am lazy, I do not want to get up this morning, but I must get up, make an effort. I do not want to do something but I must. See how extraordinary it is that we cannot catch the significance of this immediately. It has to be explained, explained, explained. We seem to be incapable of direct perception of the difference between concentration and attention; unable to have an insight into attention and be attentive.

When does attention take place? Obviously not through effort. When one makes an effort to be attentive, it is an indication that one is inattentive and is trying to make that inattention become attention. But to have quick insight, to see instantly the falseness of all religious organizations, so that one is out of them. To see instantly that the observer is the observed and therefore one makes no effort, it is so. Effort exists when there is division. Does it not indicate that one's brain has become dull because one has been trained, trained, so it has lost its pristine quickness, its capacity to see directly without all the explanations and words, words, words. But unfortunately one has to go into this because one's mind, one's brain, cannot, for example grasp instantly, that truth has no path; it is unable to see the immensity of that statement, the beauty of it and put aside all paths so that one's brain becomes extraordinarily active. One of the difficulties is that one has become mechanical. If one's brain is not extraordinarily alive and active it will gradually wither away. Now one's brain has to think, it has to be active, if only partially, but when the computer can take over all the work and most of the thought, operating with a rapidity which the brain cannot, then the brain is going to wither. This is happening, it is not an exaggerated statement of the speaker, it is happening now and we are unaware of it.

In concentration there is always a centre from which one is acting. When one concentrates one is concentrating for some benefit, for some deep rooted motive; one is observing from a centre. Whereas in attention there is no centre at all. When one looks at something immense — like the mountains with their extraordinary majesty, the line against the blue sky and the beauty of the valley — the beauty of it for a moment drives out the centre; one is for a second stunned by the greatness of it. Beauty is that perception when the centre is not. A child, given a toy, is so absorbed by it that he is no longer mischievous, he is completely with the toy. But he breaks the toy and he is back to himself. Most of us are absorbed by our various toys; when the toys go, we are back to ourselves. In the understanding of ourselves without the toy, without any direction, without any motive, is the freedom from specialization which makes the whole of the brain active. The whole of the brain when it is active is total attention.

One is always looking or feeling with part of the senses. One hears some music, but one never really listens. One is never aware of anything with all one's senses. When one looks at a mountain, because of its majesty, one's senses are fully in operation, therefore one forgets oneself.

When one looks at the movement of the sea or the sky with the slip of a moon, when one is aware totally, with all one's senses, that is complete attention in which there is no centre. Which means that attention is the total silence of the brain, there is no longer chattering, it is completely still — an absolute silence of the mind and the brain. There are various forms of silence — the silence between two noises, the silence between two notes, the silence between thoughts, the silence when you go into a forest — where there is the great danger of a dangerous animal, everything becomes totally silent. This silence is not put together by thought, nor does it arise through fear. When one is really frightened one's nerves and brain become still — but meditation is not that quality of silence, it is entirely different. Its silence is the operation of the whole of the brain with all the senses active. It is freedom which brings about the total silence of the mind. It is only such a mind, such a mind-brain, that is absolutely quiet — not quietness brought about by effort, by determination, by desire, by motive. This quietness is the freedom of order, which is virtue, which is righteousness in behaviour. In that silence alone is there that which is nameless and timeless. That is meditation.

26th July, 1981

8

Most unfortunately there are only two talks and so it is
necessary to condense what we have to say about the
whole of existence. We are not doing any kind of
propaganda; we are not persuading you to think in one
particular direction, nor convince you about anything —
we must be quite sure of that. We are not bringing
something exotic from the East like the nonsense that
goes on in the name of the gurus and those people who
write strange things after visiting India — we do not
belong to that crowd at all. And we would like to point out
that during these two talks we are thinking together, not
merely listening to some ideas and either agreeing or
disagreeing with them; we are not creating arguments,
opinions, judgements, but together — I mean together,
you and the speaker — we are going to observe what the
world has become, not only in the West but also in the
East where there is great poverty, great misery, with
enormous over-polulation, where the politicians, as here
in the West, are incapable of dealing with what is
happening. All politicians are thinking in terms of
tribalism. Tribalism has become glorified nationalism.
We cannot therefore rely on any politicians, on any
leaders, or on any books that have been written about
religion. We cannot possibly rely on any of these people,
nor on the scientists, the biologists, or the psychologists.
They have not been able to solve our human problems. I
am quite sure you agree to all that. Nor can we rely on any

of the gurus who unfortunately come to the West and exploit people and get very rich, they have nothing whatsoever to do with religion.

Having said all this it is important that we, you and the speaker, think together. We mean by thinking together not merely accepting any kind of opinion or evaluation but observing together, not only externally what is happening in the world, but also what is happening to all of us inwardly, psychologically. Externally, outwardly, there is great uncertainty, confusion, wars, or the threat of war. There are wars going on now in some parts of the world; human beings are killing each other. That is not happening in the West, here, but there is the threat of nuclear war, and the preparation for war. And we ordinary human beings do not seem to be able to do anything about all that. There are demonstrations, terrorism, hunger strikes and so on. There is one tribal group against another and the scientists are contributing to that, and the philosophers, though they may talk against it, are inwardly continuing to think in terms of nationalism, according to their own particular careers. So that is what is actually going on in the outward world, which any intelligent human being can observe.

And inwardly, in our own minds and in our own hearts, we ourselves are also very confused. There is no security, not only, perhaps, for ourselves but for the future generation. Religions have divided human beings as the Christians, the Hindus, the Muslims, and the Buddhists. So considering all this, observing objectively, calmly without any prejudice, it is naturally important that together we think about it all. Think together, not having opinions opposing other sets of opinions, not having one conclusion against another conclusion, one ideal against another ideal, but rather thinking together and seeing what we human beings can do. The crisis is not in the economic world, nor in the political world; the crisis is in consciousness. I think very few of us realise this. The crisis is in our mind and in our heart; that is, the crisis is in our consciousness. Our consciousness is our whole existence. With our beliefs, with our conclusions, with our nationalism, with all the fears that we have, it is our pleasures, the apparently insoluble problems and the thing that we call love, compassion; it includes the problem of death — wondering if there is anything hereafter, anything beyond time, beyond thought and if there is something eternal: that is the content of our consciousness.

That is the content of the consciousness of every human being, in whatever part of the world he lives. The content of our consciousness is the common ground of all humanity. I think this must be made very clear right from the beginning. A human being living in any part of the world suffers, not only physically but also inwardly. He is uncertain, fearful, confused, anxious without any sense of deep security. So our consciousness is common to all mankind. Please do listen to this. You may be hearing this for the first time so please do not discard it. Let us investigate it together, let us think about it together, not when you get home but now: your consciousness, what you think, what you feel, your reactions, your anxiety, your loneliness, your sorrow, your pain, your search for something that is not merely physical but goes beyond all thought, is the same as that of a person living in India or Russia or America. They all go through the same problems as you do, the same problems of relationship with each other, man, woman. So we are all standing on the same ground of consciousness. Our consciousness is common to all of us and therefore we are not individuals. Please do consider this. We have been trained, educated, religiously as well as scholastically, to think that we are individuals, separate souls, striving for ourselves, but that is an illusion because our consciousness is common to all mankind. So we are mankind. We are not separate individuals fighting for ourselves. This is logical, this is rational, sane. We are not separate entities with separate psychological content, struggling for ourselves, but we are, each one of us, actually the rest of human kind.

Perhaps you will accept the logic of this intellectually, but if you feel it profoundly then your whole activity undergoes a radical change. That is the first issue we have to think about together: that our consciousness, the way we think, the way we live, some perhaps more comfortably, more affluently, with greater facility to travel than others, is inwardly, psychologically, exactly similar to that of those who live thousands and thousands of miles away.

All is relationship, our very existence is to be related. Observe what we have done with our relationships with each other, whether intimate or not. In all relationship there is tremendous conflict, struggle — why? Why have human beings, who have lived for over a million years, not solved this problem of relationship? So let us this morning think together about it. Let us observe together actually what the relationship between a man and a woman is. All society is based on relationship. There is no society if there is no relationship, society then becomes an abstraction.

One observes that there is conflict between man and woman. The man has his own ideals, his own pursuits, his own ambitions, he is always seeking success, to be somebody in the world. And the woman is also struggling, also wanting to be somebody, wanting to fulfil, to become. Each is pursuing his or her own direction. So it is like two railway lines running parallel, never meeting, except perhaps in bed, but otherwise — if you observe closely — never actually meeting psychologically, inwardly. Why? That is the question. When we ask why, we are always asking for the cause; we think in terms of causation, hoping that if we could understand the cause then perhaps we would change the effect.

So we are asking a very simple but very complex question: why is it that we human beings have not been able to solve this problem of relationship though we have lived on this earth for millions of years? Is it because each one has his own particular image put together by thought, and that our relationship is based on two images, the image that the man creates about her and the image the woman creates about him? So in this relationship we are as two images living together. That is a fact. If you observe yourself very closely, if one may point out, you have created an image about her and she has created a picture, a verbal structure, about you, the man. So relationship is between these two images. These images have been put together by thought. And thought is not love. All the memories of this relationship with each other, the pictures, the conclusions about each other, are, if one observes closely without any prejudice, the product of thought; they are the result of various remembrances, experiences, irritations and loneliness, and so our relationship with each other is not love but the image that thought has put together. So if we are to understand the actuality of relationships we have to understand the whole movement of thought, because we live by thought; all our actions are based on thought, all the great buildings, the cathedrals, churches, temples and mosques of the world are the result of thought. And everything inside these religious buildings — the figures, the symbols, the images — are all the invention of thought.

There is no refuting that. Thought has created not only the most marvellous buildings and the contents of those buildings, but it has also created the instruments of war, the bomb in all its various forms. Thought has also produced the surgeon and his marvellous instruments, so delicate in surgery. And thought has also produced the carpenter, his study of wood and the tools he uses. The contents of a church, the skill of a surgeon, the expertise of the engineer who builds a beautiful bridge, are all the result of thought -- there is no refuting that. So one has to examine what thought is and why human beings live on thought and why thought has brought about such chaos in the world — war and lack of relationship with each other — and examine the great capacity of thought with its extraordinary energy. We must also see how thought has, through millions of years, brought such sorrow for mankind. Please observe this together, let us examine it together. Do not just oppose what the speaker is saying, but examine what he is saying together so that we understand what is actually happening to all of us human beings, for we are destroying ourselves.

Thought is the response of the memory of things past; it also projects itself as hope into the future. Memory is knowledge; knowledge is memory of experience. That is, there is experience, from experience there is knowledge as memory, and from memory you act. From that action you learn, which is further knowledge. So we live in this cycle — experience, memory, knowledge, thought and thence action — always living within the field of knowledge.

What we are talking about is very serious. It is not something for the weekend, for a casual listening, it is concerned with a radical change of human consciousness. So we have to think about all this, look together, and ask why we human beings, who have lived on this earth for so many millions of years, are still as we are. We may have advanced technologically, have better communication, better transportation, hygiene and so on, but inwardly we are the same, more or less — unhappy, uncertain, lonely, carrying the burden of sorrow endlessly. And any serious man confronted with this challenge must respond; he cannot take it casually, turn his back on it. That is why these meetings are very, very serious because that is why we have to apply our minds and our hearts to finding out if it is possible to bring about a radical mutation in our consciousness and therefore in our action and behaviour.

Thought is born of experience and knowledge, and there is nothing sacred whatsoever about thought. Thinking is materialistic, it is a process of matter. And we have relied on thinking to solve all our problems in politics and religions and in our relationships. Our brains, our minds, are conditioned, educated to solve problems. Thinking has created problems and then our brains, our minds, are trained to solve them with more thinking. All problems are created, psychologically and inwardly, by thought. Follow what is happening. Thought creates the problem, psychologically; the mind is trained to solve problems with further thinking, so thought in creating the problem then tries to solve it. So it is caught in a continuous process, a routine. Problems are becoming more and more complex, more and more insoluble, so we must find out if it is at all possible to approach life in a different way, not through thought because thought does not solve our problems; on the contrary thought has brought about greater complexity. We must find out — if it is possible or not — whether there is a different dimension, a different approach, to life altogether. And that is why it is important to understand the nature of our thinking. Our thinking is based on remembrance of things past — which is thinking about what happened a week ago, thinking about it modified in the present, and projected into the future. This is actually the movement of our life. So knowledge has become all-important for us but knowledge is never complete. Therefore knowledge always lives within the shadow of ignorance. That is a fact. It is not the speaker's invention or conclusion, but it is so.

Love is not remembrance. Love is not knowledge. Love is not desire or pleasure. Remembrance, knowledge, desire and pleasure are based on thought. Our relationship with each other, however near, if looked at closely, is based on remembrance, which is thought. So that relationship — though you may say you love your wife or your husband or your girl friend — is actually based on remembrance, which is thought. And in that there is no love. Do you actually see that fact? Or do you say, 'What a terrible thing to say. I do love my wife' — but is that so? Can there be love when there is jealousy, possessiveness, attachment, when each one is pursuing his own particular direction of ambition, greed and envy, like two parallel lines never meeting? Is that love?

I hope we are thinking together, observing together, as two friends walking along a road and seeing what is around us, not only what is very close and immediately perceived, but what is in the distance. We are taking the journey together, perhaps affectionately, hand in hand — two friends amicably examining the complex problem of life, neither of them leader or guru, because when one sees actually that our consciousness is the consciousness of the rest of mankind, then one realises that one is both the guru and the disciple, the teacher as well as the pupil, because all that is in one's consciousness. That is a tremendous realisation. So as one begins to understand oneself deeply one becomes a light to oneself and not dependent on anybody, on any book or on any authority — including that of the speaker — so that one is capable of understanding this whole problem of living and of being a light to oneself.

Love has no problems and to understand the nature of love and compassion with its own intelligence, we must understand together what desire is. Desire has extraordinary vitality, extraordinary persuasion, drive, achievement; the whole process of becoming, success, is based on desire — desire which makes us compare ourselves with each other, imitate, conform. It is very important in understanding the nature of ourselves to understand what desire is, not to suppress it, not to run away from it, not to transcend it, but to understand it, to see the whole momentum of it. We can do that together, which does not mean that you are learning from the speaker. The speaker has nothing to teach you. Please realise this. The speaker is merely acting as a mirror in which you can see yourself. Then when you see yourself clearly you can discard the mirror, it has no more importance, you can break it up.

To understand desire requires attention, seriousness. It is a very complex problem to understand why human beings have lived on this extraordinary energy of desire as on the energy of thought. What is the relationship between thought and desire? What is the relationship between desire and will? We live a great deal by will. So what is the movement, the source, the origin, of desire? If one observes oneself one sees the origin of desire; it begins with sensory responses; then thought creates the image and at that moment desire begins. One sees something in the window, a robe, a shirt, a car, whatever it is — one sees it, sensation, then one touches it, and then thought says, 'If I put on that shirt or dress how nice it will look' — that creates the image and then begins desire. So the relationship between desire and thought is very close. If there were no thought there would only be sensation. Desire is the quintessence of will. Thought dominates sensation and creates the urge, the desire, the will, to possess. When in relationship thought operates — which is remembrance, which is the image created about each other by thought — there can be no love. Desire, sexual or other forms of desire, prevent love — because desire is part of thought.

We should consider in our examination the nature of fear because we are all caught in this terrible thing called fear. We do not seem to be able to resolve it. We live with it, become accustomed to it, or escape from it through amusement, through worship, through various forms of entertainment, religious and otherwise. Fear is common to all of us, whether we live in this tidy, clean country, or in India where it is untidy, dirty and over-populated. It is the same problem, fear, which man has lived with for thousands and thousands of years and which he has not been able to resolve. Is it possible — one is asking this question most seriously — is it at all possible to be totally, completely, free of fear, not only the physical forms of fear but the much more subtle forms of inward fear — conscious fears and the deep undiscovered fears which we have never even known were there? Examination of these fears does not mean analysis. It is the fashion to turn to the analyst if you have any problem. But the analyst is like you and me, only he has a certain technique. Analysis implies there is an analyser. Is the analyser different from that which he analyses? Or is the analyser the analysed? The analyser is the analysed. That is an obvious fact. If I am analysing myself, who is the analyser in me who says, 'I must analyse'? It is still the analyser separating himself from the analysed and then examining that which is to be analysed. So the analyser is that which he is analysing. They are the same. To separate them is a trick played by thought. But when we observe, there is no analysis; there is merely the observing of things as they are — the observing of that which actually is, not analysing that which is, because in the process of analysing we can deceive ourselves. If you like to play that game you can, and go on endlessly until you die, analysing, and never bringing about a radical transformation within yourself. Whereas to look at the present as it is — not as a Dutchman, an Englishman, or a Frenchman or as this or that — to see what is actually happening, is pure observation of things as they are.

To observe what fear is, is not to examine the cause of fear, which implies analysis and going further and further back into the origin of fear. It is to learn the art of observing and not translating or interpreting what you observe, but just observing, as you would observe a lovely flower. The moment you take it to pieces the flower is not. That is what analysis does. But observe the beauty of a flower, or the evening light in a cloud, or a tree by itself in a forest, just observe. So similarly, we can observe fear and what is the root of fear — not the various aspects of fear.

We are asking if it is at all possible to be free of fear, absolutely. Psychologically, inwardly, what is the root of fear? What does fear mean? Does not fear arise from something that has given you pain in the past which might happen again in the future? Not what might happen now because now there is no fear. You can see for yourself that fear is a time process. Something that happened last week, an incident which brought psychological or physical pain, and from that there is fear that it might happen again tomorrow. Fear is a movement in time; a movement from the past through the present, modifying the future. So the origin of fear is thought. And thought is time, it is the accumulation of knowledge through experience, the response of memory as thought, then action. So thought and time are one; thought and time are the root of fear. That is fairly obvious. It is so.

Now it is not a question of stopping thought or time. Of course it would be impossible to stop them because the entity who says, 'I must stop thought' is part of thought. So the idea of stopping thought is absurd. It implies a controller who is trying to control thought and such a controller is created by thought. Please just observe this; *observation is an action in itself*, it is not that one must do something about fear. I wonder if you understand this?

Suppose I am afraid about something or other, darkness, my wife running away, loneliness, or this or that. I am frightened, deeply. You come along and explain to me the whole movement of fear, the origin of fear, which is time. I had pain; I went through some accident or incident that caused pain, that is recorded in the brain, and the memory of that past incident produces the thought that it might happen again, and therefore there is fear. So you have explained this to me. And I have listened very carefully to your explanation, I see the logic of it, the sanity of it, I do not reject it; I listen. And that means that listening becomes an art. I do not reject what you are saying, nor accept, but I observe. And I observe that what you tell me about time and thought, is actual. I do not say, 'I must stop time and thought', but having had it explained to me, I just observe how fear arises, that it is a movement of thought, time. I just observe this movement and do not move away from it, I do not escape from it but live with it, look at it, put my energy into looking. Then I see that fear begins to dissolve because I have done nothing about it, I have just observed, I have given my whole attention to it. That very attention is like bringing light on fear. Attention means giving all your energy in that observation.

Why is it that man pursues pleasure? Please ask yourself why. Is pleasure the opposite of pain? We have all had pain of different kinds, both physical and psychological. Psychologically, most of us from childhood have been wounded, hurt; that is pain. The consequence of that pain has been to withdraw, to isolate oneself so as not to be further hurt. From childhood, through school, by comparing ourselves with somebody else who is more clever, we have hurt ourselves, and others have hurt us through various forms of scolding, saying something brutal, terrorising us. And there is this deep hurt with all its consequences, which are isolation, resistance, more and more withdrawal. And the opposite of that we think is pleasure. Pain and the opposite of it is pleasure. Is goodness the opposite of that which is not good? If goodness is the opposite, then that goodness contains its own opposite. Therefore it is not good. Goodness is something totally separate from that which is not goodness. So is pleasure something opposite to pain? Is it a contrast? We are always pursuing the contrast, the opposite. So one is asking, is pleasure entirely separate, like goodness, from that which is not pleasurable? Or is pleasure tainted by pain? When you look closely at pleasure it is always remembrance, is it not? You never say when you are happy, 'How happy I am', it is always after; it is the remembrance of that which gave you pleasure, like a beautiful sunset, the glory of an evening, full of that extraordinary light, it gave great delight. Then that is remembered and pleasure is born. So pleasure is part of thought too — it is so obvious.

95

The understanding of relationship, fear, pleasure and sorrow, is to bring order in our house. Without order you cannot possibly meditate. Now the speaker puts meditation at the end of the talk because there is no possibility of right meditation if you have not put your house, your psychological house, in order. If the psychological house is in disorder, if what you are is in disorder, what is the point of meditating? It is just an escape. It leads to all kinds of illusions. You may sit cross-legged or stand on your head for the rest of your life but that is not meditation. Meditation must begin with bringing about complete order in your house — order in your relationships, order in your desires, pleasures and so on.

One of the causes of disorder in our life is sorrow. This is a common factor, a common condition, in all human beings. Everyone goes through this tragedy of sorrow, whether in the Asiatic world or in the Western world. Again this is a common thing we all share. There is not only so-called personal sorrow but there is the sorrow of mankind, the sorrow which wars have brought about — five thousand years of historical records and every year there has been a war, killing, violence, terror, brutality, the maiming of people, people who have no hands, no eyes — the horrors and the brutality of wars which have brought incalculable misery to mankind. It is not only one's own sorrow but the sorrow of mankind; the sorrow of seeing a man who has nothing whatsoever, just a piece of cloth, and for the rest of his life he is going to be that way — not so much in these Western countries, but in the Asiatic world it is like that. And when you see that person there is sorrow. There is also sorrow when people are caught in illusion, like going from one guru to another, escaping from themselves. It is a sorrow to oberve this, the clever people going off to the East, writing books about it, finding some guru — so many fall for that nonsense. There is the sorrow that comes when you see what the politicians are doing in the world — thinking in terms of tribalism. There is personal sorrow and the vast cloud of the sorrow of mankind. Sorrow is not something romantic, sentimental, illogical; it is there. We have lived with this sorrow from time measureless, and apparently we have not resolved this problem. When we suffer we seek consolation, which is an escape from the fact of sorrow. When there is that grief, you try every form of amusement and escape, but it always is there. Apparently humanity has not resolved it. And we are asking the question: is it possible to be free of it completely? Not avoiding it, not seeking consolation, not escaping into some fanciful theory, but is it possible to live with it. Understand those words 'to live with it': they mean not to let sorrow become a habit. Most people live with sorrow, with nationalism, which is most destructive, they live with their own separate religious conclusions, they live with their own fanciful ideas and ideals, which all again bring conflict. So live with something, live with sorrow, not accepting it, not becoming habituated to it — but look at it, observe it without any escape, without any question of trying to go beyond it, just 'hold it in your hand' and look. Sorrow is also part of the tremendous sense of loneliness: you may have many friends, you may be married, you may have all kinds of things, but inwardly there is this feeling of complete loneliness. And that is part of sorrow. Observe that loneliness without any direction, without trying to go beyond it, without trying to find a substitute for it; live with it, not worship it, not become psychotic about it, but give all your attention to that loneliness, to that grief, to that sorrow.

It is a great thing to understand suffering because

97

where there is freedom from sorrow there is compassion. One is not compassionate as long as one is anchored to any belief, to any particular form of religious symbol. Compassion is freedom from sorrow. Where there is compassion there is love. With that compassion goes intelligence — not the intelligence of thought with its cunning, with its adjustments, with its capacity to put up with anything. Compassion means the ending of sorrow and only then is there intelligence.

19th September, 1981

9

We are like two friends sitting in the park on a lovely day talking about life, talking about our problems, investigating the very nature of our existence, and asking ourselves seriously why life has become such a great problem, why, though intellectually we are very sophisticated, yet our daily life is such a grind, without any meaning, except survival — which again is rather doubtful. Why has life, everyday existence, become such a torture? We may go to church, follow some leader, political or religious, but the daily life is always a turmoil, though there are certain periods which are occasionally joyful, happy, there is always a cloud of darkness about our life. And these two friends, as we are, you and the speaker, are talking over together in a friendly manner, perhaps with affection, with care, with concern, whether it is at all possible to live our daily life without a single problem. Although we are highly educated, have certain careers and specialisations yet we have these unresolved struggles, the pain and suffering, and sometimes joy and a feeling of not being totally selfish.

So let us go into this question of why we human beings live as we do, going to the office from nine until five or six for fifty years, and always the brain, the mind, constantly occupied. There is never a quietness, there is never peace, but always this occupation with something or other. And that is our life. That is our daily, monotonous, rather lonely, insufficient life. And we try to escape from it through religion, through various forms of entertainment. At the end of the day we are still where we have been for thousands and thousands of years. We seem to have changed very little, psychologically, inwardly. Our problems increase, and always there is the fear of old age, disease, some accident that will put us out. So this is our existence, from childhood until we die, either voluntarily or involuntarily die. We do not seem to have been able to solve that problem, the problem of dying. Especially as one grows older one remembers all the things that have been, the times of pleasure, the times of pain, and of sorrow, and of tears. Yet always there is this unknown thing called death of which most of us are frightened. And as two friends sitting in the park on a bench, not in this hall with all this light, which is rather ugly, but sitting in the dappling light, the sun coming through the leaves, the ducks on the canal and the beauty of the earth, let us talk this over together. Let us talk it over together as two friends who have had a long serious life with all its trouble, the troubles of sex, loneliness, despair, depression, anxiety, uncertainty, a sense of meaninglessness — and at the end of it always death.

In talking about it, we approach it intellectually — that is, we rationalise it, say it is inevitable, not to fear it or escape from it through some form of belief in the hereafter, or reincarnation, or, if you are highly intellectual, telling yourself that death is the end of all things, of our existence, our experiences, our memories, be they tender, delightful, plentiful; the end also of pain and suffering. What does it all mean, this life which is really, if we examine it very closely, rather meaningless? We can, intellectually, verbally, construct a meaning to life but the way we actually live has very little meaning. Living and dying is all we know. Everything apart from that is theory,

100

speculation; meaningless pursuit of a belief in which we find some kind of security and hope. We have ideals projected by thoughts and we struggle to achieve them. This is our life, even when we are very young, full of vitality and fun, with the feeling that we can do almost anything; but with youth, middle and old age supervening, there is always this question of death.

You are not merely, if one may point out, listening to a series of words, to some ideas, but rather together, I mean together, investigating this whole problem of living and dying. And either you do it with your heart, with your whole mind, or else partially, superficially — and so with very little meaning.

First of all we should observe that our brains never act fully, completely; we use only a very small part of our brain. That part is the activity of thought. Being in itself a part, thought is incomplete. The brain functions within a very narrow area, depending on our senses, which again are limited, partial; the whole of the senses are never free, awakened. I do not know if you have experimented with watching something with all your senses, watching the sea, the birds and the moonlight at night on a green lawn, to see if you have watched partially or with all your senses fully awakened. The two states are entirely different. When you watch something partially you are establishing more the separative, egotistically centred attitude to living. But when you watch that moonlight on the water making a silvery path with all your senses, that is with your mind, with your heart, with your nerves, giving all your attention to that observation, then you will see for yourself that there is no centre from which you are observing.

Our ego, our personality, our whole structure as an individual, is entirely put together from memory; we are memory. Please, this is subject to investigation, do not accept it. Observe it, listen. The speaker is saying that the 'you', the ego, the 'me', is altogether memory. There is no spot or space in which there is clarity — you can believe, hope, have faith, that there is something in you which is uncontaminated, which is god, which is the spark of that which is timeless, you can believe all that, but that belief is merely illusory. All beliefs are. But the fact is that our whole existence is entirely memory, remembrances. There is no spot or space inwardly which is not memory. You can investigate this; if you are enquiring seriously into yourself you will see that the 'me', the ego, is all memory, remembrances. And that is our life. We function, live, from memory. And for us, death is the ending of that memory.

Am I speaking to myself or are we all together in this? The speaker is used to talking in the open, under trees, or in a vast tent without these glaring lights, then we can have an intimate communication with each other. As a matter of fact there is only you and I talking together, not this enormous audience in a vast hall, but you and I sitting on the banks of a river, on a bench, talking over this thing together. And one is saying to the other, we are nothing but memory, and it is to that memory that we are attached — my house, my property, my experience, my relationship, the office or the factory I go to, the skill I like being able to use during a certain period of time — I am all that. To all that, thought is attached. That is what we call living. And this attachment creates all manner of problems; when we are attached there is fear of losing; we are attached because we are lonely with a deep abiding loneliness which is suffocating, isolating, depressing. And the more we are attached to another, which is again memory, for the other is a memory, the more problems

102

there are. I am attached to the name, to the form; my existence is attachment to those memories which I have gathered during my life. Where there is attachment I observe that there is corruption. When I am attached to a belief, hoping that in that attachment there will be a certain security, both psychologically as well as physically, that attachment prevents further examination. I am frightened to examine when I am greatly attached to something, to a person, to an idea, to an experience. So corruption exists where there is attachment. One's whole life is a movement within the field of the known. This is obvious. Death means the ending of the known. It means the ending of the physical organism, the ending of all the memory which I am, for I am nothing but memory — memory being the known. And I am frightened to let all that go, which means death. I think that is fairly clear, at least verbally. Intellectually you can accept that logically, sanely; it is a fact.

The Asiatic world believes in reincarnation, that is that the soul, the ego, the 'me', which is a bundle of memories, will be born next time to a better life if they behave rightly now, conduct themselves righteously, live a life without violence, without greed and so on, then in the next reincarnation they will have a better life, a better position. But a belief in reincarnation is just a belief because those who have this strong belief do not live a righteous life today. It is just an idea that the next life will be marvellous. They say that the quality of the next life must correspond to the quality of the present life. But the present life is so tortuous, so demanding, so complex, that they forget the belief, and struggle, deceive, become hypocrites, and accept every form of vulgarity. That is one response to death, believing in the next life. But what is it that is going to reincarnate? What is it that will continue?

103

What is it that has continuity in our present daily life? It is the remembrance of yesterday's experiences, pleasures, fears, anxieties, and that continues right through life unless we break it and move away from that current.

Now the question is: is it possible, while one is living, with all the energy, capacity and turmoil, to end, for example, attachment? Because that is what is going to happen when you die. You may be attached to your wife or husband, to your property. You may be attached to some belief in god which is merely a projection, or an invention, of thought, but you are attached to it because it gives a certain feeling of security however illusory it is. Death means the ending of that attachment. Now while living, can you end voluntarily, easily, without any effort, that form of attachment? Which means dying to something you have known — you follow? Can you do this? Because that is dying together with living, not separated by fifty years or so, waiting for some disease to finish you off. It is living with all your vitality, energy, intellectual capacity and with great feeling, and at the same time for certain conclusions, certain idiosyncrasies, experiences, attachments, hurts to end, to die. That is, while living, also live with death. Then death is not something far away, death is not something that is at the end of one's life, brought about through some accident, disease or old age, but rather an ending to all the things of memory — that is death, a death not separate from living.

Also we should consider as two friends sitting together on the banks of a river, with the clear water flowing — not muddied, polluted water — seeing the movement of the waves pursuing each other down the river, why religion has played such a great part in people's lives from the most ancient of times until today? What is a religious mind, what is it like? What does the word 'religion' actually

104

mean? Because historically civilizations have disappeared, and new beliefs have taken their place, which have brought about new civilizations and new cultures — not the technological world of the computers, the submarines, the war materials, nor the businessmen, nor the economists, but religious people throughout the world have brought about a tremendous change. So one must enquire together into what we mean by 'religion'. What is its significance? Is it mere superstition, illogical and meaningless? Or is there something far greater, something infinitely beautiful? To find that, is it not necessary — we are talking this over together as two friends — is it not necessary to be free of all the things which thought has invented about religion?

Man has always sought something beyond the physical existence. He has always searched, asked, suffered, tortured himself, to find out if there is something which is not of time, which is not of thought, which is not belief or faith. To find that out one must be absolutely free, for if you are anchored to a particular form of belief, that very belief will prevent investigation into what is eternal — if there is such a thing as eternity which is beyond all time, beyond all measure. So one must be free — if one is serious in the enquiry into what religion is — one must be free of all the things that thought has invented about that which is considered religious. That is, all the things that Hinduism, for example, has invented, with its superstitions, with its beliefs, with its images, and its ancient literature such as the Upanishads — one must be completely free of all that. If one is attached to all that then it is impossible, naturally, to discover that which is original. You understand the problem? If my mind, my brain is conditioned by Hindu superstitions, beliefs, dogmas and idolatory, with all the ancient tradition, then it is anchored to that and cannot move, it is not free. Similarly, one must be free totally from all the inventions of thought, the rituals, dogmas, beliefs, symbols, saviours and so on of Christianity. That may be rather more difficult, that is coming nearer home. But all religions, whether Christian, Muslim, Hindu, Buddhist, are the movement of thought continued through time, through literature, through symbols, through things made by the hand or by the mind — and all that is considered religious in the modern world. To the speaker that is not religious. To the speaker it is a form of illusion, comforting, satisfying, romantic, sentimental but not actual.

Religion must affect the way we live, the significance of life, for then only is there order in our life. Order is something that is totally disassociated from disorder. We live in disorder — that is, in conflict, contradiction, saying one thing, doing another, thinking one way and acting in another way; that is contradiction. Where there is contradiction, which is division, there must be disorder. And a religious mind is completely without disorder. That is the foundation of a religious life — not all the nonsense that is going on with the gurus with their idiocies.

It is a most extraordinary thing how many gurus have come to see the speaker, some of them because they think I attack them. They want to persuade me not to attack, they say what you are saying and what you are living is the absolute truth, but it is not for us because we must help those people who are not as fully advanced as you are. You see the game they play — you understand? So one wonders why some Western people go to India, follow these gurus, get initiated — whatever that may mean — put on different robes and think they are very religious. But strip them of their robes, stop them and enquire into them, and they are just like you and me.

So the idea of going somewhere to find enlightenment, of changing your name to some Sanskrit name, seems strangely absurd and romantic, without any reality — but thousands are doing it. Probably it is a form of amusement without much meaning. The speaker is not attacking. Please let us understand that: we are not attacking anything, we are just observing — observing the absurdity of the human mind, how easily we are caught; we are so gullible.

A religious mind is a very factual mind; it deals with facts, with what is actually happening with the world outside and the world inside. The world outside is the expression of the world inside; there is no division between the outer and the inner. A religious life is a life of order, diligence, dealing with that which is actually within oneself, without any illusion, so that one leads an orderly, righteous life. When that is established, unshakeably, then we can begin to enquire into what meditation is.

Perhaps that word did not exist in the Western world, in its present usage until about thirty years or so ago. The Eastern gurus have brought it over here. There is the Tibetan meditation, Zen meditation, the Hindu meditation, the particular meditation of a particular guru — the yoga meditation, sitting cross legged, breathing — you know all that. All that is called meditation. We are not denigrating the people who do all this. We are just pointing out how absurd meditation has become. The Christian world believes in contemplation, giving themselves over to the will of god, grace and so on. There is the same thing in the Asiatic world, only they use different words in Sanskrit, but it is the same thing — man seeking some kind of everlasting security, happiness, peace, and not finding it on earth, hoping that it exists somewhere or other — the desperate search for something imperishable

— the search of man from time beyond measure.

So we should enquire together, deeply, into what meditation is and whether there is anything sacred, holy — not the thing that thought has invented as being holy, that is not holy. What thought creates is not holy, is not sacred, because it is based on knowledge, and how can anything that thought invents, being incomplete, be sacred? But all over the world we worship that which thought has invented.

There is no system, no practice but the clarity of perception of a mind that is free to observe, a mind which has no direction, no choice. Most systems of meditations have the problem of controlling thought. Most meditation, whether the Zen, the Hindu, the Buddhist, the Christian, or that of the latest guru, tries to control thought; through control you centralise, you bring all your energy to a particular point. That is concentration, which means that there is a controller different from the controlled. The controller is thought, memory, and that which he is controlling is still thought — which is wandering off, so there is conflict. You are sitting quietly and thought goes off; you are like a schoolboy looking out of the window and the teacher says, 'Don't look out of the window, concentrate on your book.' We have to learn the fact that the controller is the controlled. The controller, the thinker, the experiencer, are, we think, different from the controlled, from the movement of thought, from the experience. But if we observe closely, the thinker *is* the thought. Thought has made the thinker separate from thought, who then says, 'I must control.' So when you see that the controller is the controlled you totally remove conflict. Conflict exists only when there is the division. Where there is the division between the observer, the one who witnesses, the one who experiences and that which

108

he observes and experiences, there must be conflict. Our life is in conflict because we live with this division. But this division is fallacious, it is not real, it has become our habit, our culture, to control. We never see that the controller is the controlled.

So when one realises that fact — not verbally, not idealistically, not as a Utopian state for which you have to struggle, actually in one's life that the controller is the controlled, the thinker is the thought — then the whole pattern of one's thinking undergoes a radical change and there is no conflict. That change is absolutely necessary if one is meditating because meditation demands a mind that is highly compassionate, and therefore highly intelligent, with an intelligence which is born out of love, not out of cunning thought. Meditation means the establishment of order in one's daily life, so that there is no contradiction; it means having rejected totally all the systems of meditation so that one's mind is completely free, without direction; so that one's mind is completely silent. Is that possible? Because one is chattering endlessly; the moment one leaves this place one will start chattering. One's mind will continue everlastingly occupied, chattering, thinking, struggling, and so there is no space. Space is necessary to have silence, for a mind that is practising, struggling, to be silent is never silent. But when it sees that silence is absolutely necessary — not the silence projected by thought, not the silence between two notes, between two noises, between two wars, but the silence of order — then in that silence, truth, which has no path to it, exists. Truth that is timeless, sacred, incorruptible. That is meditation, that is a religious mind.

20th September, 1981

109

Krishnamurti Foundation Trust Ltd.
24 Southend Road, Beckenham, Kent BR3 1SD. England

Krishnamurti Foundation of America,
P.O. Box 216, Ojai, California 93023, U.S.A.

Krishnamurti Foundation India,
'Vasanta Vihar', 64/5 Greenways Road, Madras 600028,
India

Fundacion Krishnamurti Hispanoamericana,
P.O. Box 1782, San Juan, Puerto Rico 00919-1782, U.S.A.